SHIPWRECKS

—— OF ——

STELLWAGEN BANK

DISASTER IN NEW ENGLAND'S
NATIONAL MARINE SANCTUARY

MATTHEW LAWRENCE, DEBORAH MARX
AND JOHN GALLUZZO

FOREWORD BY JAMES P. DELGADO

THE
History
PRESS

Published by The History Press
Charleston, SC 29403
www.historypress.net

Front cover: Evening shipping on Boston Bay, 1898. The steamer *Portland* passing the pilot schooner *Columbia*. *Oil painting by maritime historical artist William G. Muller, www. WilliamGMuller.com, collection of the Minnesota Marine Art Museum.*

Back cover: A diver hovers over *Paul Palmer*'s windlass, now partially buried on Stellwagen Bank. *Matthew Lawrence, NOAA/SBNMS.*

First published 2015

Manufactured in the United States

ISBN 978.1.62619.804.3

Library of Congress Control Number: 2015935120

CONTENTS

CONTENTS

FOREWORD

Massachusetts is home to some of the most significant reminders of America's heritage. A distinguished array of historic sites, museums, archives and libraries attests to the rich tapestry of shared history and culture that reaches back thousands of years and spans the saga of what is now Massachusetts from the first peoples, the colonial era and the birth and growth of the United States. A key part of that saga is tied to the sea, from famous vessels like the *Mayflower*, the USS *Constitution*, the *Nantucket* lightship, the battleship USS *Massachusetts*, the ill-fated *Andrea Gail* or Longfellow's storied schooner *Hesperus* to the largely anonymous and very important craft that worked these waters and this coast. Gloucester schooners; fishing sloops; China and Northwest Coast fur traders; stone-, ice-, brick- and produce-laden coasters; excursion steamers; ferries; tugs; clippers; whalers; and steam packets all engaged in a rich and varied maritime trade that saw Salem and Boston emerge as America's first great ports, opening the new nation to global trade, as well as becoming a key junction in the coastal trade of the United States.

It is more than a story of ships and boats and trade. It is the story of people—those who chose and those who had no choice but to go to sea or to work on the docks and waterfronts in a variety of maritime trades. It is the story of the maritime landscape, not only that captured romantically by Winslow Homer or Fitz Henry Lane but also the gritty, grimy reality of warehouses, shipyards, canneries and coal sheds. It is the story of lighthouses, customhouses, lifesaving stations, naval bases and depots. It ultimately is the story of how we, as Americans, as human beings, interact with the sea and how it influences us as we, in turn, work to shape and change it to our needs. It is the story of how out there, on the water, we face those things that make us human, responding to the cold, cruel sea, which gives us life as surely as it takes it away.

In the pages that follow, you will take a tour of another of Massachusetts' great museums. This one rests at the bottom of the sea, off the coast in the waters of Stellwagen Bank National Marine Sanctuary. Here, in an area rich in history in the lee of Cape Cod, the sanctuary encompasses a significant part of the larger Gulf of Maine, from plankton to great whales. It also is a repository for lost ships. Some are famous, like the tragic steamer *Portland*. Others are lesser known except by the families associated with their stories, like the schooner *Lamartine* or the dragger *Edna G*. You will, in the pages that follow, come to better know these and other vessels, as well as the people who built, worked on, journeyed onboard and occasionally died in these ships.

The other part of the story is of those who now venture into the depths to rediscover these lost ships. Recreational divers, researchers, archaeologists and families all unite in the quest to find and learn more. NOAA's Office of National Marine Sanctuaries, which manages Stellwagen Bank sanctuary for the public, is committed to preserving the shipwrecks for future generations but also to working with partners in the community to share what is learned. In doing so, we connect modern audiences with the forgotten past, to the contributions of ordinary people often caught up in extraordinary circumstances and to why a shattered vessel on the bottom of the sea reflects not just our history but also that which makes us special. It is another reason why the United States created special places in the sea like Stellwagen Bank National Marine Sanctuary.

JAMES P. DELGADO, PhD
Director of Maritime Heritage
NOAA's Office of National Marine Sanctuaries

ACKNOWLEDGEMENTS

Many individuals and organizations provided support on the water, under water and in the library to make this book possible. Our gratitude to the historians, archivists, archaeologists, technicians, divers, fishermen, friends and colleagues who over the past fifteen years helped uncover Stellwagen Bank sanctuary's secrets knows no bounds. In particular, efforts to locate and document sanctuary shipwrecks would not have been successful without Ivar Babb, Kevin Joy and the team at the Northeast Underwater Research, Technology and Education Center at the University of Connecticut (NURTEC-UConn).

Within NOAA's Office of National Marine Sanctuaries (ONMS), recognition for supporting the sanctuary's maritime heritage research is due to ONMS director Daniel J. Basta, Maritime Heritage Program (MHP) director James P. Delgado and past MHP directors Timothy Runyan and John Broadwater. ONMS archaeologist Bruce Terrell has been a willing and helpful advocate, providing critical guidance along the way. The authors are grateful for the support of Stellwagen Bank sanctuary superintendent Craig MacDonald, deputy superintendent Benjamin Cowie-Haskell, all of the sanctuary's generous staff and the captain and crew of the R/V *Auk*. Sanctuary maritime heritage research would not have been possible without financial support from NOAA's Preserve America Initiative and NOAA's Office of Ocean Exploration and Research.

The New England dive community has greatly contributed to the search for Stellwagen Bank sanctuary shipwrecks. We are grateful to Heather

ACKNOWLEDGEMENTS

Knowles and Dave Caldwell of Northern Atlantic Dive Expeditions, Inc. (NADE), for their passion to explore shipwrecks and educate the local community about their finds. Likewise, great appreciation is held for Bob Foster and his team for sharing their sanctuary discoveries. Sanctuary volunteer divers Doug Costa and Chad Smith were always willing to get in the water and go for a dive.

Our sincere thanks to the following individuals and organizations that provided assistance and inspiration to delve deeper into our shared maritime experience: Arne Carr and John Fish of American Underwater Search and Survey; Victor Mastone, director of the Massachusetts Board of Underwater Archaeological Resources; David Robinson of David S. Robinson & Associates, Inc.; Dr. Brendan Foley of Woods Hole Oceanographic Institution; Dr. Erika Martin-Seibert of the National Park Service; Paul McCarthy; Captains Phil Cusumano and Bill Lee; Nathan Lipfert of the Maine Maritime Museum; the Mellinger family; Mystic Seaport Museum's Collections Research Center; Garry Kozak and Rob Morris of Edgetech; Andy Wilby of Raytheon's Applied Signal Technologies; and the captain and crew of the R/V *Connecticut*. Lastly, without the encouragement from family, the authors would not have taken the path that led to this book. We dedicate this book to you for your love and support.

The authors' proceeds from the sale of this book will go to the National Marine Sanctuary Foundation to support future maritime heritage research and interpretation at Stellwagen Bank National Marine Sanctuary.

INTRODUCTION

Some of the most well-preserved remnants of our past lie on the seafloor in the form of shipwrecks. Sunken vessels provide windows into the past that let us explore and understand our maritime legacy. America's maritime focus, its extensive inland waterways and access to the Atlantic and Pacific Oceans allowed the nation to grow and prosper through local and global maritime connections. Massachusetts' sailors and merchants were prime players at the heart of a transportation network from the first European settlement in the area. For over four hundred years, ship-borne trade, migration and fishing passed through the mouth of Massachusetts Bay, crossing what is now Stellwagen Bank National Marine Sanctuary. Vessels of all shapes and sizes carried New Englanders between Cape Cod and Cape Ann to destinations far and wide. Tragically, many of these voyages came to an unfulfilled end with the loss of many lives and much property. Today, the physical remains of hundreds of these voyages now lie on the seafloor as tangible connections to our past. Designated by the U.S. Congress to preserve, protect and interpret this nation's maritime legacy, Stellwagen Bank National Marine Sanctuary is like an underwater museum off the Massachusetts coast where fish now inhabit vessels once occupied by brave mariners and archaeological research reveals untold stories.

New England's Museum in the Sea

Stellwagen Bank National Marine Sanctuary

Office of National Marine Sanctuaries

Stellwagen Bank National Marine Sanctuary is one of fourteen special underwater places, encompassing more than 170,000 square miles of U.S. marine and Great Lakes waters, managed for the American public by the National Oceanic and Atmospheric Administration's (NOAA) Office of National Marine Sanctuaries. Similar to underwater national parks, national marine sanctuaries include some of the nation's most iconic underwater areas. The first national marine sanctuary was designated in 1975 to protect the Civil War ironclad USS *Monitor*, sunk off Cape Hatteras, North Carolina. National marine sanctuaries on America's East Coast range from New England's Stellwagen Bank to the coral reefs of the Florida Keys around to Flower Garden Banks sanctuary in the Gulf of Mexico. Sanctuaries surrounding the Channel Islands off Southern California and Washington's Olympic Coast bookend a series of special ocean places along the West Coast. Far in the Pacific, there are sanctuaries in American Samoa's waters and in the Hawaiian Islands, including the Papahānaumokuākea Marine National Monument. Each sanctuary is unique, representing important biological and/or cultural aspects. The Office of National Marine Sanctuaries' mission is to protect and enhance these natural and cultural treasures for future generations through research, management and education. National marine

NATIONAL MARINE SANCTUARY SYSTEM

The National Marine Sanctuary System encompasses fourteen of America's special underwater places. *NOAA/ONMS.*

sanctuaries encourage visitors to experience the countless opportunities for exploration, recreation and contemplation.

In 1992, the U.S. Congress designated an 842-square-mile area at the mouth of Massachusetts Bay as the tenth national marine sanctuary. The Gerry E. Studds Stellwagen Bank National Marine Sanctuary (SBNMS) is named in honor of the influential Massachusetts congressman and ocean advocate who authored the National Marine Sanctuaries Reauthorization and Improvement Act of 1992. The sanctuary encompasses Stellwagen Bank and Basin, Tillies Bank and Basin and the southern portion of Jeffreys Ledge. Its open-ocean scenic beauty, located between Cape Ann and Cape Cod, hides shallow banks and deep basins that create varied habitats supporting a rich diversity of marine life, including twenty-two species of marine mammals and more than eighty species of fish. The sanctuary is a special place held in trust for the American public; as such, sanctuary regulations afford historical resources protection unavailable in other federal waters off Massachusetts. Sanctuary regulations prohibit moving, removing or injuring or any attempt to move, remove or injure a sanctuary historical resource, including shipwrecks, artifacts and other submerged archaeological sites.

Federal legislation requires that the Office of National Marine Sanctuaries inventory, manage and interpret the National Marine Sanctuary System's historic properties, including archaeological sites, building understanding of this nation's past and linking those stories to local communities today. Most of the American maritime experience has representation in the

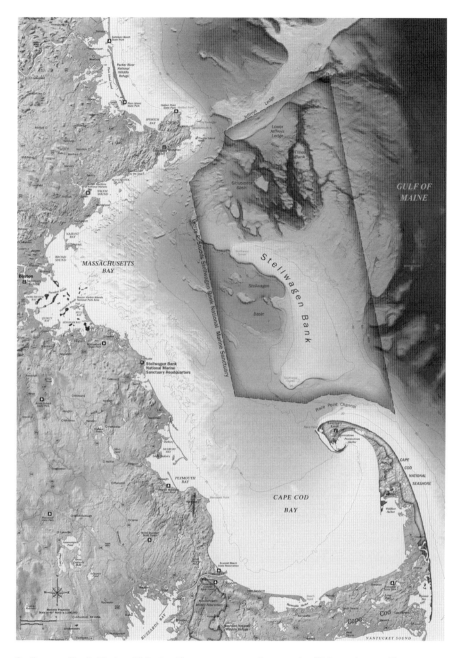

Stellwagen Bank National Marine Sanctuary spans the mouth of Massachusetts Bay between Cape Ann and Cape Cod. *NOAA/ONMS.*

National Marine Sanctuary System, allowing for a holistic approach to studying and interpreting the nation's maritime landscape.

In 2002, NOAA's Office of National Marine Sanctuaries established the Maritime Heritage Program to help sanctuaries meet their historic preservation mandates and promote maritime heritage appreciation throughout the entire nation. The program created a structure with personnel designated at individual sanctuaries and at NOAA headquarters working to support local, regional and national initiatives. These projects range from surveys to locate shipwrecks to creating exhibits with local museums. The Maritime Heritage Program links together all sanctuaries in the system through a common bond and promotes the enjoyment and appreciation of not only physical resources like shipwrecks but also intangible items like oral histories and traditional knowledge held by indigenous cultures. Maritime heritage adds a human dimension to the National Marine Sanctuary System, connecting people to their watery world and creating stewards for this blue planet.

WHEN MAMMOTHS ROAMED STELLWAGEN BANK

Stellwagen Bank National Marine Sanctuary has a rich and diverse collection of shipwrecks due to its lengthy Euro-American maritime tradition; however, humanity has had a much longer relationship with the area. Native Americans likely visited Stellwagen Bank sanctuary when lowered sea levels exposed dry land following the last ice age. Around twenty thousand years ago, the Laurentide ice sheet extended across northern North America, reaching as far south as Nantucket. This ice sheet locked away tremendous quantities of water, lowering global sea levels as much as one hundred meters. A warming period beginning eighteen thousand years ago caused the ice sheet to recede north, uncovering the continental shelf. While the area's climate was not as warm as it is today, Stellwagen Bank's environment was similar to present-day Cape Cod, with lakes, swamps, marshes and beaches. Spruce and poplar trees, as well as grasses, likely covered Stellwagen Bank and supported grazing mammals that ranged in size from small deer to mastodons. Fishermen have found the teeth of these massive animals in their nets hauled in Stellwagen Bank's vicinity. It's likely that Paleoamericans also hunted marine mammals along the shoreline for food and raw materials for clothing, shelter and tools. During this time, Stellwagen Bank was connected to Cape Cod, creating a peninsula that sheltered a shallow sea to its west, while Jeffreys Ledge projected into the Atlantic connected to Cape Ann in the north. One of the nation's oldest and largest Paleoamerican inhabitation sites lies at Bull Brook in Ipswich, Massachusetts, not far from the sanctuary's northwestern corner. Archaeologists have hypothesized that Paleoamericans may have hunted caribou along the coastal margins and possibly onto Jeffreys Ledge.[1]

Exactly how long Stellwagen Bank and Jeffreys Ledge remained connected to their respective capes has yet to be determined. Roughly ten thousand years ago, the melting and retreating ice sheet raised sea levels further, inundating Stellwagen Bank. As water slowly covered the bank, wind, currents and waves reshaped the bank's glacial deposits through erosion and re-deposition. While this process destroyed Stellwagen Bank's rich littoral environment, Native American communities did not lack for resources, as the rich marine ecosystem rimming Massachusetts Bay provided for increasingly complex cultures. Potentially, Native Americans may have returned to sanctuary waters in pursuit of marine mammals. Archaeological investigations at Caddy Park in Quincy, Massachusetts, revealed a whale tail atlatl weight, stone tools for boat building and even long blades that might have been used to butcher animals with thick layers of blubber.[2]

SANCTUARY EXPLORATION AND EXPLOITATION

Europeans likely first entered into Stellwagen Bank sanctuary's maritime history in the late sixteenth century, when fishing vessels from France, England and Portugal likely sheltered behind Cape Ann after being blown off the Grand Banks. These fishermen undoubtedly recognized the bounty available from the Gulf of Maine's productive waters, leading to official explorations by Bartholomew Gosnold, Martin Pring and John Smith. These initial forays paved the way for the European colonization of New England and the establishment of the English colony at Plymouth, Massachusetts, with the arrival of the *Mayflower* in 1620. From that period on, the region became a locus for a variety of human maritime activities. Fishery resources harvested from Stellwagen Bank played an important role as a trade commodity that ensured the success of the early English settlements. The abundance of cod, mackerel and herring allowed colonists to fish relatively close to shore from small sailing vessels such as pinks and shallops. A vital trading network soon developed that spanned the Atlantic world and formed the basis for the

John Smith's map of New England, reprinted in 1635, indicated good fishing grounds on Stellwagen Bank. *Map reproduction courtesy of the Norman B. Leventhal Map Center at the Boston Public Library.*

region's maritime-based economy. An abundance of timber and access to deep-water ports also ushered in the beginning of a lucrative shipbuilding industry that prospered well into the nineteenth century.

European maritime conflict created opportunities for New England's colonial merchant fleet to trade with the Atlantic world. While hostile blockades of America's ports during the American Revolutionary War and the War of 1812 created temporary impediments to free-flowing maritime trade that originated in Massachusetts' maritime communities and spanned the globe, fishing remained one of the most lucrative ventures, and the ports of Gloucester, Boston and Provincetown were some of the top places to land one's catch taken off Stellwagen Bank. Whaling also provided New Englanders with a valuable export commodity. Initially, large pods of right whales inhabited the waters surrounding Stellwagen Bank. The animals' seasonal proximity to shore allowed fishermen to hunt them using rowed small boats. As the inshore

Like generations before him, a Portuguese dory fisherman hand lines for cod off Cape Cod in 1942. *Library of Congress, FSA/OWI Collection, LC-USW38-002175-E.*

fishery overexploited the local whale population, whalers sailed farther out into the Atlantic to hunt their quarry. During the nineteenth century, whaling activities became a global enterprise, where large ships pursued whales into the vast reaches of the Pacific Ocean. Oftentimes, these voyages took two or more years, ending only when the hold was full of whale oil. The whaleship would then return to one of the many ports around Massachusetts Bay and sell its hard-earned cargo to Boston merchants for export.

New England developed its cultural identity through its maritime interaction with other societies around the globe. This cultural exchange was made possible by the international trading and whaling voyages that originated and returned to communities on the sanctuary's doorstep.

The Provincetown whaling steamer *A.B. Nickerson* hunted fin whales in Massachusetts Bay near Stellwagen Bank. *Fall River Marine Museum.*

Vessels from Boston, Salem and other Massachusetts ports transited through the sanctuary on the way to the Far East, Europe and the Caribbean. In addition to the commodities exchanged with Europe, tens of thousands of Europeans immigrated to the United States on vessels that passed through the sanctuary's waters on the way to Boston.

Increasing maritime traffic in the nineteenth century, expansion of the American nation and development of the U.S. federal government led to efforts to make waterborne movement of goods and people safer. Created in 1807, the U.S. Coast Survey, a predecessor to NOAA and the nation's first science agency, was responsible for charting America's waterways to reduce shipping casualties and guide mariners in and out of busy ports. From the seventeenth century onward, coastal fishermen and mariners were aware of the underwater bank spanning the mouth of Massachusetts Bay. Not only was "Middle Bank" a productive fishing ground, but it also provided a navigation check to those transiting into the bay in low visibility. Scientific charting of "Middle Bank" was finally undertaken by Lieutenant Henry S. Stellwagen, on loan to the Coast Survey from the U.S. Navy, who was dispatched to the area to assess lighthouse and lifesaving station locations. In the fall of 1854, while in command of the USCSS *Bibb*, his survey party used a sounding lead and careful navigation to establish the bank's extents, surrounding depths and sediment composition. Superintendent of the Coast Survey Alexander Bache rewarded Stellwagen for his efforts by naming the bank after him. Almost a century and a half later, U.S. Geological Survey and Canadian Hydrographic Service hydrographers mapped the entire sanctuary with multi-beam sonar, revealing every small depression and ridge and even shipwrecks. The research team also named two topographic features, Creed Basin and Creed Ridge, after its survey ship CCGS *Frederick G. Creed*.

U.S. Navy lieutenant Henry Stellwagen led the expedition that scientifically mapped "Middle Bank" in 1854. *U.S. Navy History and Heritage Command.*

MARITIME ARCHAEOLOGY: UNCOVERING STELLWAGEN BANK SANCTUARY'S SECRETS

At the time of the sanctuary's designation, NOAA had only a limited understanding of the number of shipwrecks in the area, and not a single geographic position was known to the government managers. After comprehensive mapping of the sanctuary's seafloor with multi-beam sonar revealed a number of potential wrecks, sanctuary staff began to actively investigate the sanctuary's maritime heritage. Since 2000, the sanctuary's shipwreck inventory has grown to fifty vessels, ranging from nineteenth-century schooners to modern fishing trawlers. Investigating these shipwrecks has resulted in a better understanding of the region's maritime landscape. Archival sources indicate that approximately two hundred more shipwrecks are awaiting discovery.

Maritime archaeology is the study of the physical remains of humanity's interaction with the oceans, lakes and rivers focusing on vessels, shore-side facilities, cargos, artifacts and submerged landscapes. Maritime archaeological sites, in the form of shipwrecks, usually represent a defined period in time rather than a slow deposition of material accumulated over a period of years; thus, many describe shipwrecks as time capsules. Underwater archaeological sites often have better preservation of organic artifacts as compared to land sites, allowing researchers to learn more about the past. NOAA archaeologists conduct yearly surveys to expand the sanctuary's site inventory, allowing them to interpret the beautiful and dramatic shipwrecks that document New England's maritime history.

Discovering shipwrecks in Stellwagen Bank sanctuary requires extensive survey work utilizing remote sensing tools. Since the sanctuary sits out in the open ocean with no submerged obstructions or land for vessels to run into, it can be difficult to pinpoint where a vessel sank from the historical record. Sinking accounts often give only a rough description, with little detail to help narrow down the search area. Thus, position uncertainty combined with the sanctuary's cold and murky depths that range from sixty-five to over five hundred feet create a largely opaque layer best penetrated by acoustic imaging systems.

Maritime archaeologists most frequently employ side-scan sonar to search for sanctuary shipwrecks. A side-scan sonar system includes a topside computer connected by a long cable to a towfish pulled at depth by a research vessel. The towfish transmits sound pulses and receives the pulse's echoes off the seafloor and any items that project above it. The echoes are converted into digital data that is transmitted up the tow cable and back to a topside computer, where it is saved and graphically displayed in real time. Archaeologists analyze the data and determine if the towfish has pinged a man-made object, such as a shipwreck, or natural features, like piles of rocks. Magnetometers are another often-used tool; when towed near the seafloor, they detect variations in the earth's magnetic field that might be caused by a shipwreck's iron or other magnetic materials. A magnetometer can detect anchors, cannons and machinery and is particularly helpful when this material is buried and undetectable with the side-scan sonar.

Once archaeologists have located remote sensing targets, they often need to take a closer look to be sure the targets are actually shipwrecks. Sanctuary researchers use SCUBA (self-contained underwater breathing apparatus) to slip below the ocean's surface and examine shipwrecks firsthand. Outfitted with double tanks and dry suits, researchers brave the chilly forty-five-degree-Fahrenheit water to document the shipwreck with cameras, measuring tapes, slates and pencils. This information is then analyzed and compared to the

A sanctuary archaeologist prepares a side-scan sonar and magnetometer for deployment. *Matthew Lawrence, NOAA/SBNMS.*

An NOAA SCUBA diver waits to be picked up by the R/V *Auk* after a visit to a shallow sanctuary shipwreck. *Matthew Lawrence, NOAA/SBNMS.*

NURTEC-UConn technicians lower the ROV *Kraken 2* into the water to explore shipwrecks in deeper waters. *Matthew Lawrence, NOAA/SBNMS.*

historical record to learn when the vessel was in service and maybe even its name. Sanctuary divers limit their investigations to targets found in less than 130 feet of water and depend on underwater robots called remotely operated vehicles, or ROVs, to go deeper. Tethered to the surface with an umbilical that transmits power, data and imagery, ROVs "fly" through the water with thrusters, allowing archaeologists to examine sanctuary shipwrecks at any depth. ROVs let archaeologists spend hours examining a shipwreck, warm and dry onboard a research vessel, to determine the characteristics that may help identify it.

Stellwagen Bank National Marine Sanctuary's collection of shipwrecks and maritime heritage stories represents a vibrant part of this nation's connection to the ocean. From accounts of the War of 1812 sea battle between USS *Chesapeake* and HMS *Shannon* to whale hunts and rumrunners anchored on Stellwagen Bank during Prohibition, these events and activities have shaped our past and can again enrich the lives of current and future generations.

2

THE *PORTLAND* GALE'S FURY

1898's PERFECT STORM

New England's maritime history is intimately linked with the coastal storms that have lashed its seaside communities. While the individual impact on families who lost property or family members was felt deeply by those involved, in most cases, storms have left ephemeral marks on the seaside inhabitants who faced their fury. Each subsequent storm experienced by the current generation has pushed the storm stories of previous generations from the public's consciousness. The February 1802 storm that wreaked havoc on the fishing and trading fleets anchored in Massachusetts Bay harbors fled the memories of those who weathered the December 1839 storms. While the relative severity of these storms was difficult to judge across the decades, the process of experience replacement was hastened by limited communication and access to written recollections.

Interestingly, the *Portland* Gale of 1898 has not faded from memory in the same fashion as other storms. Occurring as it did at the cusp of the twentieth century, with increasing levels of media coverage, the dramatic stories of human loss captured the attention of readers nationwide. As decades passed and subsequent storms like the Great Hurricane of 1938 battered New England, historian and raconteur Edward Rowe Snow stepped into the story and became a troubadour of popular maritime history, carrying the story to new generations. At the center of the *Portland* Gale story is the steamship *Portland*, a night boat and coastal passenger steamer integral to New England's maritime transportation network. The story of this vessel's loss with all passengers and crew provided the dramatic thread to captivate

Debris from the *Portland*, including its helm, washed ashore on the outer Cape Cod beaches. *Edward Rowe Snow Collection, Howard Gotlieb Archival Research Center at Boston University.*

new generations. However, the *Portland*'s story is multifaceted and much broader than the notoriety of its demise. It connects to the beginnings of coastal steam navigation in New England, continuing a transportation system that brought Boston and Portland, Maine, closer together.

NIGHT BOATS IN NEW ENGLAND

The inception of New England coastal steam navigation in the 1820s brought greater connectivity between port cities, but slow vessel speeds necessitated overnight passages between ports. Technological advances in steam navigation during the 1830s and 1840s allowed steamships to become true night boats, departing port in the evening and arriving at the destination the following morning. The night boat's layout included main deck space for cargo, a dining area and saloon for passengers and passenger staterooms on the upper decks. Passenger cabins overhung the steamship's hull on paddle guards, otherwise known as sponsons, which projected outward, increasing the vessel's beam.

Night boats were more than physical structure; the fare structure of these lines was also similar. A low, basic fare covered passage, with additional fees for berthing and meals. The geographical range of night boats was also similar from line to line. Each trip covered approximately 125 to 200 miles. Longer routes developed in the late nineteenth and early twentieth centuries as steamship design and engine technology progressed to allow a much faster voyage.

The first steamer characterized as a night boat, *James Kent*, operated between New York City and Albany in 1823. Steam navigation's development from the 1830s to the 1850s resulted in four main night boat lines in New England: the New York–New London Line, the Stonington Line, the Old Bay Line and the Fall River Line. Remarkably, all of these lines survived into the twentieth century. From the 1850s to the turn of the century, night boats were an integral component of the passenger transportation network between New York and ports in southern New England or from Boston to Maine's Down East cities.

Night boats of the later nineteenth century competed favorably against or worked in conjunction with overnight train service in New England. The steamship's luxurious accommodations and service compensated for its slightly slower speed between destinations. Furthermore, steamship passengers could dine on excellent fare and sleep in cabins and berths as comfortable as hotel rooms. The night boat's cheap fares also attracted passengers away from rail service and onto the water. Steamship companies and railroads often worked together to supply through tickets to destinations, making long-distance travel easier. During the 1890s, the competition for passengers between rail and night boats was evenly matched, but by the 1900s, train travel had taken over a majority of the passenger trade between cities. Professor of economics at UCLA George W. Hilton felt that, "partly because of the flamboyant architecture of the large boats, and partly because of the heavy travel on the major lines, the night boat was a more conspicuous part of the American transportation system than its quantitative importance warranted."[3]

In 1823, Captain Seaward Porter and Boston business interests chartered the Kennebec Steam Navigation Company to run the steamship *Patent* between Boston and Bath, with stops in Portland each way. The *Patent's* first 110-mile, sixteen-hour voyage marked the beginning of continuous night boat connection between Boston, New England's industrial center, and Portland, the up-and-coming center of transportation and trade in Maine. Within a few short years, the Kennebec Steam Navigation Company folded, leaving Porter with possession of the *Patent*, which he continued to operate between Boston and Portland with more success than before. Would-be competitors, witnessing the success of Porter's *Patent*, attempted to run steamers from Boston to Portland, but their efforts ultimately failed, providing Porter with a selection of steamers to expand his business. Initially, the vessels were small and unsuited for the route, as they originated from calmer inland waterways.[4] Mechanical problems and other mishaps resulting from unfamiliarity with steam machinery aside, these early steamers managed to show New England merchants and businessmen that regular and direct service between the two cities was warranted and desired.

In 1835, Captain Porter's Eastern Steamboat Company contracted for the construction of the *Portland*, the first steamship specifically designed for the Boston–Portland route. The 146-foot-long steamer linked the cities until 1842, when a direct rail link between Boston and Portland by the Eastern Railroad moved it to a coastal Maine route. The combined forces of the Eastern Steamboat Company and the Eastern Railroad started a period of intense competition with Menemon Sandford's steamboat lines resulting in the temporary end of Boston–Portland steamship service in 1843. In response, a group of Boston and Portland shipping interests organized the Portland Steam Packet Company to connect the cites.[5]

Chartered in 1844 with its main offices in Portland, the newly formed company capitalized on the higher railroad rates and rails' inability at that time to carry bulk cargo with the screw steamers *Commodore Preble* and *General Warren*. The line's steamers traveled between the ports six nights a week and maintained a lower travel cost than the railroad, but the line was more interested in freight shipment than passengers. Following several years of successful freight transportation, the Portland Steam Packet Company expanded its regular service with the side-wheel steamer *John Marshall*, this time focusing on transporting passengers.[6] During the next five decades, the Portland Steam Packet Company added new steamers to the line to remain competitive with the railroads and other steamship companies that sprang up on the same route.

By 1889, the Portland Steam Packet Company was in need of a new vessel. The line's 260-foot *Tremont*, built in 1883, was well furnished in the Queen Anne style, but its other vessel, the 230-foot *Forest City*, was out of date. Built in 1854, the *Forest City*'s tired accommodations and weak engine meant that it could not satisfy the public's increasing demand for luxury. The new vessel had to be palatial to meet the public's expectations in the face of greater competition arising from the consolidated rail lines of the Boston and Maine Railroad.[7]

THE *PORTLAND*'S CONSTRUCTION AND CAREER

Throughout America in the last quarter of the nineteenth century, night boat designers and shipyards transitioned to steel hulls; however, the shift to steel did not reach the shipyards of Maine, which steadfastly exploited the state's inexpensive skilled labor force to produce wooden hulls that were less expensive than steel. Not surprisingly, the Portland Steam Packet Company chose to construct a wooden-hulled side-wheel steamship. The New England Shipbuilding Company started construction on the *Portland*'s hull in March 1889 by laying its white oak keel on the banks of the Kennebec River at Bath. Work on the vessel progressed steadily throughout the summer. Shipwrights used more oak in its frames, secured together with copper-alloy bolts, and affixed iron strapping to the frames below main deck level for structural reinforcement. The steamer even had wrought-iron partitions that divided the hull into three watertight compartments for added safety at sea.

As the steamship's construction progressed, readers of the *Bath Daily Times* learned that the *Portland*'s main cabin featured a domed skylight while two octagonal skylights lit the forward saloon, an area that had two tiers of staterooms surrounding a central open gallery. Its main saloon stretched 225 feet long, with staterooms fore and aft of the paddle boxes. In total, the steamship's 167 cherry-paneled staterooms held 514 white pine berths for passengers and crew. Befitting the steamer's luxury status, its accommodations were "large, commodious, and will be elegantly finished and furnished, making it one of the most attractive and comfortable cabins possible to imagine."[8]

The shipyard launched the *Portland*'s hull on October 14, 1889, attended by one of the largest crowds to ever assemble for a Bath launching. The steamship measured 280.9 feet between perpendiculars and 291.0 feet from its cutwater to its elliptical stern. Its hull spanned 42.1 feet in breadth; however, its overhanging paddle guards spread its maximum breadth to 65.0 feet. Now afloat, tugs moved the steamer a short distance downriver to receive its twin boilers from the Bath Iron Works before it was towed on to Portland for its engine.

The steamship *Portland* docked in Boston in 1891. *Deborah Marx.*

The Portland Company fabricated and installed the massive single-cylinder walking beam engine during the winter of 1889–90. The engine was a common variety of condensing-beam steam engine, having an upright cylinder sixty-two inches in diameter with a twelve-foot stroke. Its twin, coal-fired iron boilers generated steam pressure of fifty pounds per square inch, resulting in 355 nominal horsepower from the steam engine. At this pressure, the thirty-five-foot, ten-inch-diameter paddle wheels revolved twenty times per minute, pushing the steamship along at fifteen miles per hour.[9]

At a cost of $240,000, the *Portland* represented a significant increase in capacity and luxury over its predecessors and was the largest side-wheel steamship running east of Boston at the time.[10] Its design was a compromise of carrying capacity, passenger comfort, shallow draft and construction cost. While screw propulsion was considered to be more seaworthy, Maine's side-wheel night boats had traveled New England's Down East routes with success for decades.[11]

Antonio Jacobsen's 1891 oil painting held by the Maine Historical Society provides a sense of the steamer's colorful and ostentatious decoration. A gilded stem head ornamented the steamer's cutwater, while an eagle perched on a gilded globe sat atop the pilothouse. The main deck extended from the freight deck at the bow to the ladies' saloon in the stern. The freight deck was entirely enclosed forward of the paddle wheels, creating a barrier for large seas. Extending three-quarters of the steamship's length above the freight deck and ladies' saloon, the saloon deck housed staterooms and the main saloon. The third and top level, the hurricane deck, contained the pilothouse, captain's and officers' quarters and more passenger cabins. Sited roughly amidships, twin smokestacks projected nearly as high as the steamer's main masts. Just aft of the stacks, the walking beam and top of the A-frame rose above the cabins on the hurricane deck. The *Portland*'s hull and three-level superstructure were painted white with a black band encircling the vessel at the sponson, and its paddle boxes were gold, red and black with a gilt globe and seal of the City of Portland on each side. Four lifeboats flanked each of the *Portland*'s paddle boxes on the hurricane deck, while life rafts sat atop its upper cabins.

The *Portland* departed Portland for Boston on its maiden voyage on June 14, 1890, and returned that evening, marking the start of its daily service between the two cities. Initially, the steamship operated opposite the *Tremont*, with both vessels departing opposite cities at either six or seven o'clock in the evening. In 1895, the *Portland* began running opposite the newly built steamship *Bay State*, the *Portland*'s near sister ship built by the same shipyard. At the same time the *Bay State* went into service, the *Portland* received a significant upgrade with the installation of an electric lighting plant, making it more comparable to its newer sister. Nightly trips between cities cost one dollar each way, with staterooms costing an additional one to three dollars.

The *Portland* and the *Bay State* were the best way for vacationers to reach Maine. Joint marketing between Maine's rail lines and the Portland Steam Packet Company (later renamed the Portland Steamship Company) laid out all the travel options, with the steamship line offering "the best of care and the best of fare…and equal to any hotel in the land."[12] While the wealthier vacationers chose the *Portland* for its luxury accommodations, the increasing availability and low cost of steamship and rail transportation made it feasible for people in the great commercial and industrial centers of the Northeast to spend part of their summers at Maine's seaside resorts and hunting camps. Economic growth during the Victorian era enlarged the middle class, increasing the number of people who possessed the expendable income and leisure time to take Maine vacations. New England's residents also used the *Portland* for short-term leisure travel, taking quick trips to celebrate special occasions with friends and family.

Many passengers also utilized the *Portland* for business travel. Boston was the established center of trade by the 1890s, while Portland was growing to become Maine's coastal center of manufacturing. Businessmen in New England favored the nightly run between Boston and Portland via steamship

The *Portland*'s refined accommodations made it the best way to travel for business or pleasure between Boston and Portland. *Deborah Marx.*

instead of by rail. The vessel's timely, regular service and comfortable cabins made for a relaxing overnight trip along the coast, and the steamship line offered through tickets from Boston to Providence, Springfield, Worcester, New York, Philadelphia, Baltimore and Washington.

For nearly a decade, the *Portland* connected Boston and Portland without much incident, a testament to its skilled crew who navigated the unwieldy paddle wheeler in the congested waters of Boston Harbor. Newspapers recorded only one collision in September 1895, when the *Portland* ran afoul of the excursion steamer *Longfellow* off Rowe's Wharf in Boston Harbor. Once disentangled, the *Portland* continued north with only $1,000 worth of damage, while the *Longfellow* continued to its dock with very little damage. The steamship line took advantage of its nearly pristine safety record in its advertising, boasting that "after fifty-two years of service to the traveling public, this Company, with new and powerful steamers, unrivaled passenger accommodations, careful and experienced officers in every department, will endeavor to give the same assiduous care through which, in more than half a century no passengers have lost life or received injury to person or property."[13]

THE *PORTLAND*'S WRECK AND THE STORM'S AFTERMATH

The *Portland* sailed from Boston on November 26, 1898, under the command of Hollis H. Blanchard, carrying approximately two hundred passengers and crew and a large shipment of freight. The steamship's cargo consisted of dry goods, boots, shoes, flour and general merchandise valued at $45,000. Weather reports indicated that a storm was developing south of New England, but Captain Blanchard chose to leave port at the scheduled seven o'clock in the evening departure time. It was a clear night as the *Portland* left Boston Harbor, but within hours the collision of two weather disturbances produced heavy snow and wind over ninety miles per hour. Sea conditions offshore likely deteriorated quickly as the *Portland* left the shelter of Cape Ann. Other vessels out in the storm sighted the *Portland* as it labored against the mounting seas; the last known sighting of the steamer occurred off Gloucester about eleven o'clock that night. Ultimately, the storm overcame the steamship sometime around nine o'clock the following morning, as indicated by the stopped watches found on passengers' bodies that washed

Captain Hollis H. Blanchard was an experienced mariner but new to command of the *Portland*. *Edward Rowe Snow Collection, Howard Gotlieb Archival Research Center at Boston University.*

ashore. The *Boston Evening Transcript* reported, "It is certain that the *Portland* passed Gloucester and that the gale struck her in full force near Thatcher's Island. Probably she could not have headed against the terrific blast and drifted against the wind to her doom." There were no survivors. Tragically, the Portland Steamship Company did not keep a passenger list ashore. Only through more recent historical research has the steamship's loss been tallied at either 192 or 193 passengers and crew.[14]

Bodies and wreckage from the steamer began to wash ashore on Cape Cod on the evening of November 27, 1898, and over the following several days, U.S. Life-Saving Service surfmen recovered only forty of the nearly two hundred victims. The *Boston Post* wrote, "This is the most terrible catastrophe on the record of the coastwise traffic from the port of Boston. It surpasses all in its completeness and its unexpectedness. It is especially harrowing in the number of its victims. Many a great battle does not present such a list of fatalities as this single wreck." On November 30, 1898, the *Portland's* owners officially declared the steamship a total loss with all onboard. Bodies and flotsam from the *Portland* continued to wash ashore on Cape Cod for weeks. The largest piece of wreckage located was only thirty feet in length, composed of the *Portland's* superstructure. Other pieces of debris included furniture, the main and auxiliary steering wheels and cabin woodwork; no portion of the vessel's hull floated ashore.[15]

The year 1898 was responsible for the largest number of reported shipwrecks in New England, according to maritime historian John P. Fish. His analysis of maritime disasters indicated that 1898 was a truly bad year for shipping and that the *Portland* Gale sank 70 percent of the vessels lost that year, some 380 vessels.[16] The *Portland* Gale broke all forms of land communication between Cape Cod and Boston. Snowdrifts blocked the railroad lines, and high winds had blown down the telegraph wires, preventing Cape Cod Life-Saving Service surfmen from reporting the large quantity of debris washed ashore from the steamer and other vessels. News of the storm's impact and the *Portland*'s loss finally made it to Boston, but only through the perseverance of individuals who braved the winter weather.

With the *Portland* valued at $250,000 at the time of its loss but only insured for $60,000, the Portland Steamship Company recouped some of its investment, but the families of the ship's passengers ultimately had no financial recourse in the courts. A court investigation of the catastrophe released the Portland Steamship Company and Hollis H. Blanchard from any blame. The official finding was that "[the *Portland*] foundered through an act of God."[17] The social impact on several New England communities was dramatic. Portland's African American community was particularly hard hit; nineteen of the *Portland*'s sixty-three crew members were African Americans belonging to that city's Abyssinian Meeting House. The lost crew members equaled 10 percent of the church's congregation and were in many cases the primary wage earners of extended families. The disruption in the social fabric resulting from the *Portland*'s loss fragmented Portland's African American community and led to the Abyssinian Meeting House's closure in 1916. An effort is currently underway to restore the building and use it to preserve and interpret Maine's African American heritage.

The steamship's loss also changed the practice of using wooden-hulled side-wheel steamships. The *Bay State* remained in service but was modified with smaller, feathering paddle wheels and completely enclosed paddle boxes. When the Portland Steamship Company replaced the *Portland* the following year, it purchased a steel-hulled screw steamer, *Governor Dingly*. Other steamship companies did likewise, mostly abandoning the construction of wooden shallow-draft hulls for steel hulls with a deeper draft. After the *Portland*'s loss, Maine's shipyards built only one more wooden-side paddle wheel steamship, the *Ransom Fuller*, for the Boston–Maine routes. In general, the vessels built after the *Portland*'s loss were better suited to their routes. Even with a new steel steamship, the Portland Steamship Company did not make it far into the twentieth century. The Eastern Steamship Company bought the line in 1901, when it consolidated most of the New England steamship lines.

For ninety-one years, the *Portland*'s whereabouts remained a mystery. Shortly after it sank, the *Boston Globe* funded an expedition to locate the *Portland* on the shoals immediately north of Cape Cod, but the searchers failed to produce any wreckage associated with the vessel. Local historian and author Edward Rowe Snow tried again in the 1940s; his efforts located a wreck seven miles north of Cape Cod that he felt was the *Portland*, but this claim could not be substantiated. Ultimately, better search technology allowed John P. Fish, H. Arnold Carr and Peter Sachs, the principals of the Historical Maritime Group of New England, to locate the steamship in 1989. The remote sensing experts took into account the passengers' stopped watches, debris drift patterns, tidal currents, the time and location of bodies and artifacts washed ashore on Cape Cod and where fishermen reported net hangs to narrow down the search area. Even still, the researchers spent thousands of hours systematically surveying areas north of Cape Cod with side-scan sonar and a fathometer until they finally located the *Portland*. The Historical Maritime Group returned to the shipwreck several times with remote underwater cameras to capture images of the *Portland*, but the wreck's depth and currents proved problematic. Unfortunately, the imaging technology available to the men did not allow them to capture the wide-angle imagery needed to conclusively prove that the wreck was indeed the *Portland*. In 2002, H. Arnold Carr provided Stellwagen Bank sanctuary staff with the *Portland*'s geographic coordinates, allowing the sanctuary to mount an expedition to confirm the Historical Maritime Group's find.

ARCHAEOLOGICAL SITE INVESTIGATION

Stellwagen Bank sanctuary conducted its first archaeological investigation of the *Portland* in July 2002, working with the National Undersea Research Center at the University of Connecticut (NURC-UConn), now known as the Northeast Underwater Research, Technology and Education Center at the University of Connecticut (NURTEC-UConn). Departing from Gloucester onboard the R/V *Connecticut*, the research team planned to investigate a multi-beam sonar anomaly directly adjacent to the geographic coordinates for the *Portland* provided by H. Arnold Carr. The research methodology called for a side-scan sonar survey followed by remotely operated vehicle (ROV) dives to ground truth any sonar targets. Utilizing armored tow cable spooled on a hydraulic winch, the research team first deployed an Edgetech DF1000 dual-frequency side-scan sonar. As the R/V *Connecticut* transited the survey lanes, the sonar soon revealed a large vessel upright on the seafloor with a clearly identifiable paddle guard. Sonar software measurement tools indicated that the vessel's hull was appropriately sized to be the *Portland*. The shipwreck's acoustic shadow hinted at a walking beam steam engine located

A synthetic aperture sonar image of the *Portland*'s hull. The bright dashes off its starboard side are large fish. *NOAA/SBNMS*.

amidships. Based on the side-scan sonar imagery, the research team felt that a ROV investigation was warranted.

The R/V *Connecticut* next shifted into ROV operations mode and maneuvered into position above the shipwreck, with its dynamic positioning thrusters keeping it precisely on station over the site. ROV technicians then deployed NURC-UConn's Deep Ocean Engineering Phantom III S2 ROV in tandem with a depressor weight to control the vehicle's tether. The ROV carried a video camera with scaling lasers, halogen lighting, an acoustic tracking system and sector-scanning sonar. Shortly after reaching the seafloor, the scientists watching the ROV's video monitors were rewarded with the sight of a massive wooden hull, heavily encrusted with colorful marine organisms. After rising up from the muddy bottom, the ROV explored the shipwreck's main deck along its port side, encountering several sets of bitts, a stowed anchor and copper-alloy pipes that carried the hot and cold running water for its heads. Upon reaching amidships, the ROV's lights revealed an auxiliary boiler

One of the *Portland*'s main boiler steam exhaust pipes on the seafloor off the vessel's bow. A cusk usually lives inside. *NOAA/SBNMS and NURTEC-UConn.*

and paddle wheel flanges entangled with menacing nets that caused the ROV pilot to halt the exploration.

Lastly, the team explored the seafloor just off the bow, imaging a large copper-alloy pipe with a flange at one end and a spittoon-shaped opening at the other. Measuring approximately eight feet long and eight inches in diameter, further analysis determined that the object was a boiler's steam release pipe, a common feature on steamships throughout the nineteenth century. Satisfied with this initial investigation, the team recovered the ROV and returned to Gloucester. The following day, ROV investigation continued with a focus on the vessel's stern, where the team located the *Portland*'s still-attached rudder, turned to starboard, under an overhanging elliptical stern. Ultimately, sonar imagery and underwater video of the shipwreck proved that the Historical Maritime Group had found the *Portland*'s resting place.

Historical and archaeological investigations of the *Portland* are ongoing. Since the first research mission in 2002, NOAA maritime archaeologists have surveyed a wide area around the *Portland*, uncovering a debris trail pointed toward Provincetown. Contrary to many accounts, there is no evidence that the *Portland* sank in a collision, and no other sunken vessel has been found immediately adjacent to the steamship that could have caused it to sink. Since 2002, archaeologists have returned to the shipwreck with NURTEC-UConn's ROVs on five missions to learn more about the wreck and interpret it for the public. As underwater technology improved so did the ROVs used to study the *Portland*. NURTEC-UConn's *Hela* and *Kraken 2* ROVs replaced the Phantom III vehicle and brought back stunning high-definition video and still images that revealed new details about the wreck. Following several years of fieldwork and historical research, sanctuary archaeologists nominated the *Portland* to the National Register of Historic Places based on its historical association to New England steam navigation and the *Portland* Gale. The *Portland*'s significance was also related to its very well-preserved remains and to what its shipwreck could reveal about the past. After review by the National Park Service, the *Portland* was listed on the National Register in 2005.

In addition to the research goals of past ROV missions, the sanctuary sought to share the *Portland* with the public. To that end, a television crew joined a 2003 expedition and produced a Science Channel documentary in the *Science of the Deep* series entitled "The Wreck of the *Portland*." Similarly, the NURTEC-UConn/sanctuary team connected the R/V *Connecticut* to Provincetown in 2005 with a long-range wireless computer network and broadcast live underwater video from the *Portland* to audiences at the Pilgrim Monument and Provincetown Museum and on the Internet. Viewers were able to explore the wreck alongside the research team without having to leave their armchairs.

In August and September 2008, technical SCUBA divers made their first visits to the *Portland*. Robert Foster, Vladislav Mlch, David Faye, Don Morse and Paul Blanchette undertook the highly dangerous and complex dives after several years of preparation. The divers' short bottom times of fifteen to eighteen minutes required over three hours of decompression at various depths before they could surface. The divers' mobility and spatial awareness under water allowed them to avoid derelict nets that kept the ROVs from certain areas near the steamer's engine, revealing interesting aspects of life onboard the steamship.

THE *PORTLAND*'S ARCHAEOLOGICAL REMAINS

The *Portland* lies partially embedded in a mud bottom, twenty miles off Gloucester. Its largely intact wooden hull has survived from the main deck level down to the keel and lists slightly to starboard. Pointing south toward Provincetown, ocean currents have scoured out the seafloor along the steamship's portside while sediment has accreted up the vessel's starboard side at amidships. ROV and side-scan sonar surveys of the steamer's remains revealed that almost no superstructure projected above the main deck and very little deck planking covered its stern aft of the steam engine. However, a considerable amount of deck planking still covered the freight deck forward of the engineering space. Combining the archaeological information with the historical reports of the vessel's superstructure ashore on the outer Cape Cod beaches begins to fill out a picture of the *Portland*'s last moments. Contemporary interviews of knowledgeable mariners suggest that Hollis Blanchard would have kept the steamer headed into the waves, hoping to outlast the storm. For an as yet undetermined reason, the *Portland*'s bow swung to the southeast, putting the steamer broadside to the waves piling into Massachusetts Bay from the northeast. ROV video revealed that the *Portland*'s rudder is in place and turned to starboard, possibly indicating that Captain Blanchard initiated the steamship's turn to the south near the time of its loss. The waves and screaming wind breached the superstructure, allowing water to fill the hull. The *Portland* settled quickly, larger sections of superstructure broke free and, as the steamship plunged to the bottom, compressed air pushed aft, blowing the stern superstructure and deck planking free of the hull.

One of the most fascinating aspects of the *Portland* is its intact engine. Just forward of amidships, the *Portland*'s boiler uptakes project vertically through its freight deck to a height of more than ten feet above the deck. At the uptakes' top, twin flanges connected to separate smokestacks that were likely swept off as the *Portland* sank. The seemingly undisturbed position of the uptakes and intact deck planking above its boilers do not suggest a cataclysmic boiler failure before or during the *Portland*'s plunge to the seafloor.

The *Portland*'s giant single-cylinder steam engine is positioned immediately aft of the boiler uptakes, separated by the engine control station that has yet to be explored due to entangled nets. The cylinder's crosshead slides project vertically from its top, stabilizing its piston rod. Above the cylinder, the *Portland*'s diamond-shaped walking beam rises fifty feet above the seafloor on its wooden A-frame. One question yet to be resolved is whether the connecting rod between the walking beam and paddle shaft crank is still intact. Entangled nets have thus far prevented an examination of this linkage. A broken connecting rod may indicate that the steamer lost its ability to fight the waves, and that is why it swung broadside before sinking.

Smaller artifacts lie scattered inside and outside the hull, primarily along the *Portland*'s starboard side. Stacked windowpanes, stacked plates and delicate teacups lay in an area believed to be a storeroom near the galley forward of the starboard paddle wheel. Whereas steamship china is famously

Teacups in the *Portland*'s pantry hint at what service was like on the steamship and remind us of the wreck's human toll. *NOAA/SBNMS and NURTEC-UConn.*

emblazed with the line's logo, these teacups had a simple blue and pink flower pattern. Other pieces of dishware and several oil lanterns of a variety used to light the *Portland*'s binnacle lay on the seafloor in this area as if they had spilled out from the same storeroom. Several bowls and electric lighting fixtures were incorporated into a debris pile outboard from the galley area.

Incongruously, a large shaving mug rested among the tangled water pipes near the steering gear on the freight deck. The *Portland*'s barber, William Comer, chose not to sail on that fateful evening, believing he would have few customers on what he anticipated to be a rough passage. His chair and showcase with the tools of his trade were on the main deck. From expedition to expedition, sanctuary archaeologists recorded the pipes' positions in relation to the shaving mug, noting significant changes in position beyond what could be expected from natural influences. Fishing gear impacts were suspected to have caused the pipes' movements.

The *Portland*'s remains are extremely susceptible to impacts from fishing activities, particularly bottom trawling. Its location in Gloucester Basin places it on one of the trawling routes frequented by fishermen. During one research

Twisted copper water pipes and a ceramic shaving mug lie on the *Portland*'s main deck. *NOAA/SBNMS and NURTEC-UConn.*

expedition when the R/V *Connecticut* was stationed over the wreck with the ROV exploring the wreck, a fisherman radioed the *Connecticut*'s captain, asking him to move so that the trawler could "scrape the side of the wreck." Numerous gillnets cover the steamship's hull, snagged on projecting timbers and machinery, while an entire trawl net, including doors and tow cables, hang from the *Portland*'s starboard bow. The derelict fishing gear greatly limited ROV access to the shipwreck, hampering its complete documentation.

Since all firsthand witnesses of the *Portland*'s final moments perished when the vessel sank, its shipwreck represents the only source of new information about the disaster. Locating the *Portland*'s final resting place itself rewrote nearly a century of speculation. The *Portland*'s substantially intact remains offer the chance to time travel back, not only to November 1898 but also to a time when traveling between Boston and Portland was a voyage rather than a short trip on the interstate highway.

THE *PORTLAND* GALE'S OTHER STEAMSHIP VICTIM: THE *PENTAGOET*

Linked by the churning maelstrom of the November 1898 storm, the embattled steamship *Pentagoet* fought the howling wind and mountainous seas north of Cape Cod. Race Point Life-Saving Station keeper Samuel O. Fisher noted in his journal at 5:45 a.m. on November 27 that he heard a steamship blow its whistle four times, which he interpreted as a distress signal. Many believed the whistle blasts were the *Portland*'s final moments, but the sheer distance to where the *Portland* now lies makes this unlikely. Could the *Pentagoet* have been blowing its whistle before it sank? A wreck lying on the eastern side of Stellwagen Bank, nine miles north of Cape Cod, suggested that possibility.

The *Pentagoet* went into service as the wooden-hulled steamship *Hero*. The small steamer measured 104 feet long when launched in 1864, with a simple vertical direct-acting steam engine turning its single propeller. Built in Philadelphia for commercial purposes, the U.S. government purchased the vessel from its owners, S. and J.M. Flannagan, in July and shortly thereafter commissioned the steamer at the Philadelphia Navy Yard with acting ensign James Brown in command.

Detailed to the North Atlantic Blockading Squadron and renamed *Moccasin*, the steamer took up a guard position off Fort Delaware. After sailing in pursuit of the Confederate navy cruiser *Tallahassee*, reported to be at Halifax, the *Moccasin* returned to its duty station on the Delaware River. In the spring of 1865, the *Moccasin* steamed into the Chesapeake in time for the surrender of the Army of Northern Virginia at Appomattox Court House on April 9. While many vessels in the Potomac Flotilla to which the *Moccasin* was attached were released in May, the steamship continued to operate in the area, carrying patients to Washington, D. C.'s naval hospital.[18]

The U.S. Navy decommissioned the *Moccasin* in August and sold the steamer to the Treasury Department. Reoutfitted for the Revenue Cutter Service in Baltimore, the *Moccasin* was first stationed at Norfolk, Virginia, and then moved to Wilmington, North Carolina, in 1866 and eventually to Rhode Island and Connecticut. While stationed at Stonington in August 1872, the *Moccasin* rescued survivors of the steamship *Metis*, run down off Watch Hill, Rhode Island, by the schooner *Nettie Cushing*. The *Metis*' terrified passengers and crew, numbering around 150, clambered into four lifeboats and floating debris. The *Moccasin*, men from the Watch Hill Lighthouse, lifeboat crews from the Watch Hill Life-Saving Station and local fishermen all responded to the scene, saving 33 people. The efforts of Captain David Ritchie and the *Moccasin*'s crew earned them commendations from the Massachusetts Humane Society and gold medals struck by congressional resolution.[19]

In the spring of 1881, Captain James H. Merryman prepared an order for the *Moccasin*'s refitting, to include lengthening the vessel and raising its main deck. Towed into the New York Shipyard of Slater and Reid by the *Ewing*, the *Moccasin* grew to 128 feet in length and became the USRC *George M. Bibb*. After the refit, the Treasury Department dispatched the *George M. Bibb* to Detroit, Michigan, under the command of Captain Sheppard. In the early 1880s, the *George M. Bibb* operated with the U.S. Revenue Service, checking the papers and cargos of vessels sailing Lake Huron, Lake Erie and Lake Ontario, with occasional trips to Lake Superior. By the late 1880s, the *George M. Bibb* was showing its age; the crew had to repeatedly replace planks, and its framing showed signs of rot. An 1890 board of survey condemned the vessel, and it was subsequently stricken from the government's rolls in 1890. In October 1891, it was sold to George H. Kimball of Cleveland, Ohio. Following Kimball's purchase, the vessel underwent another round of shipyard repairs in Cleveland before being sent to the East Coast a month later.[20]

Renamed the *Pentagoet* and enrolled out of Belfast, Maine, in 1892, the steamer went into service on the New York run carrying canned fish. In addition to its longer voyages, the *Pentagoet* ran local trips from Rockland to Swan's Island or Vinalhaven. Starting in 1894, the *Pentagoet*'s captain, George H. Oakes, operated the steamer between Eastport and Jersey City, New Jersey.[21]

In May 1896, not far from the site of the *Metis* disaster, the *Pentagoet* went back into the lifesaving business. En route from New York to Eastport, the *Pentagoet*'s crew rescued Captain Bullerwell and two crew members from the schooner *Willie D.*, which capsized west of Point Judith. One seaman drowned as their schooner sank, leaving the remaining sailors clinging to the capsized vessel's spars. The *Pentagoet* landed the survivors in Vineyard Haven before continuing its trip north.[22]

During another trip from Eastport to New York, Captain Oakes and the *Pentagoet*'s crew rescued Peter Byckman and his son of Bucksport, Maine, from an experimental craft that was described as operating like a coffee grinder. First sighted by the *Pentagoet*'s second officer, Andrew Haughey, eighteen miles off Mount Desert Island, Captain Oakes invited the Byckmans to travel to New York. The elder Byckman accepted the offer on the provision that his craft could be towed along; heavy seas the following day parted the towline, causing the unusual craft to be lost.[23]

Beginning in 1898, the *Pentagoet* began operating for the recently established Manhattan Steamship Company under the command of Captain F. Cates. On its last voyage, the *Pentagoet* left New York on Thursday, November 24, 1898, and headed for Rockland and then Bangor under the command of Captain Orris R. Ingraham. Captain Ingraham

The steamship *Pentagoet*'s significantly modified and aging hull was no match for the *Portland* Gale's fury. *Deer Isle–Stonington Historical Society*.

had decades of experience navigating New England's waters as pilot or master. The last of six brothers, all of whom were steamboat captains, Ingraham commanded steamers on the Fall River and Nantasket Lines before taking over from Captain Cates.

The *Pentagoet* was last sighted off Truro, Massachusetts, on Saturday afternoon, November 26, and is believed to have foundered during the high seas and strong winds that began that evening. Newspaper reports of the *Pentagoet*'s sinking were overshadowed by the *Portland*'s greater loss of life. However, the *Pentagoet*'s sailors were the second-greatest loss of life from one vessel. Without passengers, the list of the *Pentagoet*'s loss was more accurately known. In addition to Captain Ingraham, seventeen sailors perished. The *Pentagoet*'s officers hailed from Rockland, while most of its crew lived in New York. Interestingly, the steamer's steward and mess man were African Americans filling the same jobs as the *Portland*'s African American crew members.[24]

Initially, hope for the *Pentagoet*'s safe arrival was held by the Manhattan Steamship Company's general manager. To allay concerns, he telegraphed the line's agent in Bangor, saying that all expected that the *Pentagoet* had gone out to sea. Captain Otis Ingraham, Orris's twin brother and captain of the coastal steamer *City of Bangor*, was also optimistic; in addition to knowing his brother's seamanship skills, he was familiar with the *Pentagoet*'s construction. He felt that "she was so low down in the water that she could not possibly topple over, and the deck being flush offered no chance for the water to get in and sink her." Others were not as sure of the *Pentagoet*'s seaworthiness. A former officer on the *George M. Bibb* told the *Boston Globe* the story of its sale by the Revenue Cutter Service into private hands and related, "I saw the vessel many times in New York, and despite her greasy dirty look I never had any trouble in distinguishing the old *Bibb*. I boarded her once and her officers said that the new owners had not expended over $300 on the new vessel. She was a cheap job."[25] By December 3, all concerned had come to the conclusion that the *Pentagoet* was lost in the great gale, but where had it sunk? Unlike the *Portland*'s debris, which carpeted Cape Cod beaches in the days following the gale, no confirmed pieces of the *Pentagoet* washed ashore. Archaeological research may hold the answer.

INVESTIGATING THE *PENTAGOET*

Sanctuary researchers first encountered the shipwreck suspected to be the *Pentagoet*, but otherwise known as STB007, in 2000 utilizing a drop camera system to investigate multi-beam sonar anomalies. Repeated passes across the shipwreck revealed wooden hull structure, chain and small pieces of coal but otherwise a shipwreck mostly obscured by the sands of Stellwagen Bank. Returning to the site with side-scan sonar in 2002 provided archaeologists with a wide-scale view that revealed an oblong hull shape projecting mere inches from the sand. Overall, shipwreck material stretched a distance of 150 feet along the vessel's northeast-southwest longitudinal axis. Anchor chain extended 250 feet from the northeast end on the north side of the shipwreck in a sinuous arc. The sonar imagery did not provide sufficient information to determine which end of the vessel was its bow. Just southwest of the site, the sonar also revealed a furrow in the sediment little more than 160 feet from the shipwreck that represented the path of a scallop dredge that had narrowly missed the wreck.

STB007's investigation continued in 2005 with the ROV research team from NURC-UConn. Utilizing the center's *Hela* ROV, sanctuary archaeologists got a much more detailed view of the wreck. During the course of a two-hour dive, the ROV pilot maneuvered the vehicle into position to examine the features revealed by the side-scan sonar. Most of the vessel's lower hull was buried in the sand, and little hull structure above the turn of the bilge was extant. At the northeast end of the site, a large

The *Pentagoet*'s hawse pipe and anchor chain with pieces of coal in the foreground. A wolfish now resides in the tangled chain. *Heather Knowles, NADE.*

ten-inch-square iron beam projected approximately nine feet vertically from the wreckage. Covered with pink, white, orange and brown metridium anemones and sea stars, the projecting feature was likely either a stempost or sampson post. Large, eight-inch links of studlink anchor chain were wrapped repeatedly around the beam's base. Not more than twenty feet east of the beam, the ROV's lights revealed an anchor ring and fluke barely projecting from the sandy bottom, indicating the buried presence of an anchor. The anchor, anchor chain and vertical beam suggested that the site's northeast end was its bow. Seemingly contradictory clues made this determination less conclusive; at the southwest end of the site, another pile of studlink chain included the vessel's hawse pipes. Further analysis of the ROV video footage and side-scan sonar imagery suggested that the chain and hawse pipes had been dragged into their current position by a trawl net or dredge.

As the ROV pilot flew the vehicle down the vessel's length where hull edges projected from the sand, the research team noticed increasing amounts of coal in the troughs between sand waves. Unlike other coal cargo–carrying vessels explored in the sanctuary, the coal had not created a central concentrated mound, suggesting that it was not the vessel's primary cargo. Other nondescript pieces of iron also came into view, including several pieces with rivet holes suggestive of boiler plating. Longitudinal structural timbers were also seen along the vessel's centerline. Under these timbers and between the frames, piles of broken shells indicated where wolfish had taken up residence.

Prior to the sanctuary's designation in 1992, recreational divers reportedly visited the wreck and found a variety of artifacts on it. These divers named the wreck the "Christmas" or "Toy" wreck because of the assorted pieces of general merchandise found. Divers also recovered pieces of steam machinery from the wreck, and an unknown fisherman reportedly snagged a bell in his nets. Information about this site provided to the Massachusetts Board of Underwater Archaeological Resources confirmed that site STB007, visited in 2005, was the "Toy" wreck. Noted shipwreck historians John P. Fish and H. Arnold Carr located the site in the 1970s following up on fishing net hangs. One tip they received was from a Provincetown fisherman, Captain Joe Roderick, who recovered a sternpost from the site in the 1960s or early 1970s. Captain Roderick donated the sternpost, including brass gudgeons, to the Truro Historical Society, where it can be seen at the Highland House Museum. The museum attributes the sternpost to the steamship *Portland*.

While not conclusive, STB007 is thought to be the *Pentagoet* for the following reasons. The wreck's dimensions are consistent with the *Pentagoet*'s dimensions, and the presence of a limited amount of coal suggests bunker fuel rather than a full cargo. Furthermore, recovered steam machinery fragments and boiler plating found at the site indicate a steam-powered vessel. Unfortunately, the removal of artifacts from the site clouds this information source, but the variety found by divers seems to match reports of the general cargo the *Pentagoet* loaded in New York before its departure. Future archaeological research will hopefully reveal new information to solve this mystery.

3

ANCIENT ENERGY

WATERBORNE TRANSPORTATION
OF COAL

O n a clear day looking out from the sandy bluffs above the outer Cape
Cod beaches at Provincetown during the age of sail, a visitor would
have been struck by the large number of schooners of all sizes lined up
along the horizon. Favorable southwesterly winds would have let the vessels
pass just offshore of the Cape's sand bars on as direct a course as possible
to Boston. However, any resident, having seen the view countless times,
would have considered it mundane—simply the movement of coal, the
predominate cargo passing through the area during the later half of the
nineteenth century. Today, collier (coal-carrying) shipwrecks lie throughout
Stellwagen Bank sanctuary, evidence of stormy weather and human error
and emblematic of the industrialization and urbanization that created
America's densely populated New England coast. The stories of the *Frank A.
Palmer*, *Louise B. Crary* and *Paul Palmer*, now all sanctuary shipwrecks, provide
a view of the great coal schooners, the ultimate expressions of the sailing
coastwise coal trade.

Coal fields were first located in North America at Cape Breton, Nova
Scotia, in the late seventeenth century and in the early eighteenth century
along the Appalachian Mountains stretching from Pennsylvania to West
Virginia. Consumer coal use for heating was highly limited in the American
colonies; blacksmiths and iron founders used its dense energy, but wood
satisfied the needs of most people. As forests were cleared around growing
cities, firewood had to be cut and shipped longer distances, thereby increasing
its cost and the difficulty in getting it to market. Coal offered the distinct

advantage of producing considerably more heat per weight than wood. As demand for coal increased, the infrastructure to mine and transport coal likewise developed. Commercial waterborne transportation of coal began in the 1790s, when coal mines near Richmond, Virginia, shipped coal cargos to New York, Boston and Philadelphia. Small sloops and schooners engaged in the already established coasting trade between the Mid-Atlantic States and New England were perfectly suited to load a coal cargo on the James River.

By the start of the American Civil War, water power and wood could not keep up with the energy needs of industrialization and urbanization. The material needs of the Union army played a crucial role in the coal trade's growth to support manufacturing, which continued after the war along with the energy needs of expanding railroads. Anthracite coal shipped from Philadelphia made that city an important coal port after the Civil War, but the massive quantities of bituminous coal that became available in the 1880s and 1890s as a result of advances in the railroad infrastructure between the West Virginia mines and Norfolk and Newport News grew the bituminous trade to enormous levels.[26]

At the turn of the century, the emerging use of electricity further fueled the demand for coal. Coal-powered steam engines turned the dynamos

Coal, carved from a narrow Appalachian mine, begins its journey to a New England furnace. *Library of Congress, National Child Labor Committee Collection, LC-DIG-nclc-01060.*

generating power for electric lighting and electric motors. Electricity soon began to supplant more traditional uses of coal, exemplified by the installation of electric street railways in American cities. During the twentieth century, coal solidified its position in America as the dominant fuel source for electrical generation, ultimately outgrowing the capabilities of a diminishing coasting trade.[27]

RISE OF THE GREAT NEW ENGLAND COAL SCHOONERS

The North American coasting trade depended on the schooner rig to make the low margins in bulk cargo transport profitable. Economical schooners needed half the sailors as compared to a square-rig ship, brig or bark of equal tonnage. Schooner crews did not need to climb into the rigging on a regular basis; shipowners could therefore employ more inexperienced crewmen, saving on labor costs. Furthermore, a schooner was better adapted to coastwise sailing with its ability to sail closer to the wind and maneuver in tight harbors and rivers—the schooner's mostly self-controlling sails allowed it to tack with agility. The rig's simplicity also made it cheaper to build and maintain. The sum of the above advantages was a handy vessel with an economic advantage embraced by American sailors and utilized to move people and goods along the Atlantic seaboard.[28]

Prior to the 1860s, two-masted schooners had predominated in the harbors and on the shipping routes of the U.S. East Coast. Hull lengths and tonnages steadily increased, and enterprising shipbuilders in New England realized that the addition of a mast would decrease the sail area of each individual sail, making the sails easier to handle. Once a number of three-masted schooners were in service by the 1870s, shipowners found that the cost of manning these larger vessels increased little with their growth in carrying capacity. The addition of donkey boilers and steam engines to power anchor windlasses and lifting engines in the 1880s further reduced the manual labor that necessitated a larger crew.

As the end of the nineteenth century approached, the need for ever larger coal schooners was evident from the demands placed on the transportation system by New England's industries and heating requirements. The ability to build five- and six-masted wooden schooners on the East Coast was primarily limited to Maine's shipbuilders. In most other East Coast shipbuilding centers,

The Norfolk and Western coal pier in Norfolk used gravity-fed shoots to load the largest schooners. *Library of Congress, Detroit Publishing Company Collection, LC-DIG-det-4a12477.*

labor costs were too high to employ a large body of wooden shipwrights. Maine, on the other hand, had a large pool of experienced shipwrights and labor who accepted considerably lower wages.

The three-masted schooner, common by 1870, increased its carrying capacity from 500 tons to 1,100 tons. By the 1880s, the average four-master could carry 2,500 tons of coal. Between 1879 and 1955, 459 four-masted schooners sailed in the coasting trade on the U.S. East and Gulf Coasts. Bath, Maine, led the way, with 150 four-masted schooners launched into the Kennebec River alone.[29] Historian William Armstrong Fairburn wrote, "As the economic urge for size was felt, the schooners became larger and were fitted with four masts, and during the latter part of the last decade of the century, size got somewhat out of hand."[30] The four-master *Frank A. Palmer* perfectly exemplified this trend.

CONSTRUCTION OF THE *FRANK A. PALMER*

Four-masted schooner design and construction reached its apogee at Nathaniel T. Palmer's Bath shipyard. Born to a ship rigger, builder and owner in 1860, Nathaniel T. Palmer specialized in building four-masters; he launched the *Sarah E. Palmer* and *Augustus Palmer* in 1894, the *Mary E. Palmer* in 1895 and the *William B. Palmer* in 1896. Together, this fleet was known as the "First Palmer Fleet."

Nathaniel T. Palmer laid the *Frank A. Palmer*'s keel in September 1896 and launched the schooner on March 18, 1897. The vessel was very much a family affair; Nathaniel T. Palmer's niece, Grace Palmer, christened the schooner with a bouquet of roses on her seventeenth birthday, and the schooner bore the name of Nathaniel's brother, who rigged the vessel. The *Frank A. Palmer* had the latest laborsaving equipment such as a steam windlass, pumps, sounding machines and safety devices. When launched, the schooner measured 274.5 feet in length, 43.5 feet in breadth and had a 21.0-foot depth of hold. The schooner stretched 415.0 feet from the tip of its jib boom to the end of the spanker boom. A simple gammon head graced its bow, and its elliptical stern formed an elegant finish to the schooner's aft end. All told, the schooner spread over eight thousand square yards of canvas. The *Frank A. Palmer* was the longest four-masted schooner ever built and was longer and had a greater tonnage than the East Coast's first five-masted schooner, *Governor Ames*.

Topside, the *Frank A. Palmer*'s poop deck extended two-thirds of the vessel's length from the cabin trunk at the stern to forward of the main mast. Separated from the poop deck and situated on the main deck, the forward deckhouse contained the crew quarters, galley, steam lifting engine

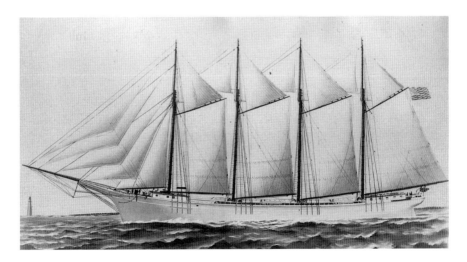

An idealized painting of the *Frank A. Palmer* sailing by Minot's Light off Massachusetts' South Shore. *Maine Maritime Museum, Bath, Maine.*

and donkey boiler. Forward of this deckhouse, an enclosed bow housed the steam-powered anchor windlass. In addition to the windlass, steam from the donkey boiler also powered gypsy heads, pumps and capstans. The aft deckhouse, or cabin trunk, was recessed into the stern aft of the poop deck and held the captain's cabin and officers' quarters. The *Frank A. Palmer*'s gray hull had a yellow stripe running from bow to stern at the main deck level, while its deckhouses, stanchions, fly rail and bowsprit were painted white. After its launch, Captain James E. Rawding took the schooner downriver from Bath on its first voyage, supported by his very able first mate, Captain Elliot Gardner, and a small but handy crew.[31]

Construction of the *Louise B. Crary*

The transition from four-masted to five-masted schooners was not a fluid development. In 1888, the Leverett Storer shipyard in Waldoboro, Maine, built the first five-master on the East Coast: the *Governor Ames*. At 245 feet long and 1,778 tons, the *Governor Ames* was not outstandingly large, but due to an older rigging style, with backstays and shrouds set up with dead eyes and lanyards, its masts came un-stepped and fell overboard on its maiden voyage. The mishap spread distrust of the design and prevented Maine shipbuilders from embracing a fifth mast until ten years later, when hull lengths necessitated a fifth mast to make the sails more manageable. Following the *Frank A. Palmer*'s launch in 1897, shipbuilder Nathaniel T. Palmer launched the East Coast's second five-masted schooner, the *Nathaniel T. Palmer*, in 1898. The schooner was clearly too large to be a four-master at 2,440 tons gross and 295 feet long. Mr. Palmer had set the dividing line between four and five masts. The *Nathaniel T. Palmer* paved the way for the adoption of a five-masted schooner rig in the New England coal trade.[32]

The New England Shipbuilding Company, builder of thirty-eight four-masted schooners, did not build nearly as many five-masters. The *Louise B. Crary*, launched at the yard on November 20, 1900, was one of only four five-masted schooners turned out by the company. A group of investors that included its captain, William H. Potter; his brother William T. Potter; the schooner's managing owner; and approximately thirty-nine others assembled the contract price of $100,000. At its launch, Mrs. Louise B. Crary, wife of Thomas B. Crary, one of the schooner's principal investors, showered its bow with American Beauty roses. However, she was not the

The *Louise B. Crary* at anchor, possibly in Vineyard Sound, with a full cargo of coal under its hatches. *Maine Maritime Museum, Bath, Maine.*

only one who christened the schooner that day. As the schooner slid down its ways, another individual standing on its bow was seen throwing sheets of paper. Upon investigating, onlookers found the papers to be Bible leaves thrown by a "Shiloh convert," who was christening the craft in accordance with the beliefs of his church.

As the *Louise B. Crary* slipped down the shipbuilding ways into the Kennebec River, it measured 267.1 feet in length and 46.2 feet in breadth; its cavernous hold had room for 3,700 tons of coal. Like the *Frank A. Palmer*, the *Louise B. Crary* was built with a "long poop" deck layout. Separated by open passageways from the poop, the forward deckhouse held the forecastle, engine room and engineers' quarters. Enclosed within the poop, the midship deckhouse accommodated the galley, mess and second mate's cabin. The aft deckhouse held cabins for the captain, first officer and guests. These cabins had hot and cold water and steam heat from the donkey boiler. The *Louise B. Crary*'s builders supplied the schooner with state-of-the-art improvements, including a Robinson Patent Steerer, Hyde steam windlass, engine and wrecking pumps. It even had patented riding stoppers for the anchor chains that reduced the jarring vibrations caused when the schooner was anchored in a seaway. Two boats, one 24.0 feet long and another 16.0 feet long, were fitted onboard to use as lifeboats or tenders.[33]

The *Frank A. Palmer*'s and *Louise B. Crary*'s Careers

The *Frank A. Palmer* and the *Louise B. Crary* followed a relatively predictable routine hauling coal along the Atlantic coast, from which they only occasionally deviated for a special cargo or port. The *Frank A. Palmer*'s first trip took it from Bath to Louisbourg, Nova Scotia, where it loaded coal for Portland, Maine. When the schooner arrived in Portland with two hundred boxcars of coal, the locals took note. It was the biggest schooner afloat, discharging the largest coal cargo ever received in that city.[34]

After offloading, the *Frank A. Palmer* returned to Louisbourg to pick up more coal for Portland. The forty-nine-hour passage from Portland was one of the quickest trips on record. Aside from these early trips north, the *Frank A. Palmer*'s voyages focused to the south over the next five years, sailing back and forth between the Chesapeake and New England transporting coal and very occasionally another bulk cargo such as railroad ties. Between 1897 and 1900, Nathaniel T. Palmer owned and managed the *Frank A. Palmer*, along with the other five schooners he built, as the "First Palmer Fleet." In 1900, Nathaniel T. Palmer sold his schooners to J.S. Winslow and Company of Portland, Maine. Jacob S. Winslow and Henry P. Dewey started the company in 1861, carrying freight in the Caribbean and oceanic trades. As the company entered its thirtieth year in business, it began operating large schooners in the New England coal trade. By this time, management of the company had shifted to Eleazer W. Clark, Winslow's brother-in-law, who grew the company into the largest fleet of sailing vessels on the East Coast. While J.S. Winslow and Company contracted with shipyards for schooners, many more were purchased from failed owners as the economic realities of the coal trade concentrated ownership of the great schooners into fewer companies.[35]

During the *Frank A. Palmer*'s five years of operation, the schooner loaded at least fifty-one coal cargos, transporting in excess of 173,400 tons from the coal terminals at Baltimore, Philadelphia, Newport News and Norfolk. The schooner visited Newport News most frequently, carrying nearly twice as many loads from its coal docks as any other port. Two-thirds of all the schooner's shipments were unloaded in Boston and Portland, while Providence, Portsmouth and Bangor received the remainder.[36]

The *Frank A. Palmer* also made several international trips, and in one instance, the schooner supported the United States Navy's involvement in the Spanish-American War. On July 21, 1898, off Santiago, Cuba, Russell Doubleday, a gunner onboard the auxiliary cruiser *Yankee*, spent three days shoveling coal from the *Frank A. Palmer*, much to his chagrin. In total, the USS *Yankee*'s sailors transferred two hundred tons of coal to their cruiser.[37] Commercial colliers sailed worldwide to fill the U.S. Navy's coalbunkers, keeping the naval ships on station closer to the action.

Beginning with its first trip in December 1900, the *Louise B. Crary* made eighteen coal trips carrying more than 66,600 tons to New England from the Chesapeake. Eleven trips originated in Newport News, and the remainder was split between Norfolk and Baltimore. Boston received most of the coal, while Providence, Portland, Portsmouth and Bangor also received shipments.[38]

A well-organized transportation system was needed to supply the coal to fill a great coal schooner's cavernous holds. Coal mined in the interior regions of the Mid-Atlantic States moved via rail to coal ports on the Chesapeake Tidewater or the Delaware River. The *Frank A. Palmer* and *Louise B. Crary* were in a continual race to load, sail and discharge. However, the vessel's speed mattered far less than the rate at which it was loaded and unloaded. Coal port loading facilities had varying levels of capacity, with the largest shipping point for the New England market being the Chesapeake and Ohio terminal in Newport News. Locomotives pushed coal-filled rail cars up tall trestles adjacent to docks, dumping the coal down folding chutes that extended from the top of the trestle into the schooner's cargo hatches. Gangs of trimmers distributed the coal to the vessel's farthest ends, ensuring maximum capacity and stability. Newport News' mechanized terminal could load and trim a five-master in twenty-four hours, but more commonly, it required six or seven days. Gravity made for easy loading at the largest ports; however, discharging the cargo was much more laborious, requiring large bucket scoops, cranes and considerable manual labor.[39]

After loading its cargo, a tug towed the schooner from the docks out into the Chesapeake Bay for its transit north. If several vessels were heading to the same port, it became a race to be the first schooner to the discharging dock. The trip north was straightforward depending on the weather. Usually, schooners sailed directly up the coast to Vineyard Sound south of Cape Cod. Unfavorable winds might cause schooners to anchor in the sound awaiting the right weather to round Cape Cod. When the weather window opened, a fleet of schooners would sail through bars and shoals of Vineyard and Nantucket Sounds, around Cape Cod and on to their final destinations. When a vessel reached port, a tug would tow the schooner into the harbor and up to the unloading docks. Returning south in ballast, coal schooners navigated more directly, still in a race with the competition. A round-trip voyage could be completed in three weeks, with a profitable coal schooner making eleven to fourteen round trips per year.

The *Frank A. Palmer* and *Louise B. Crary*, as with most great New England coal schooners, had a variety of mishaps. These ranged from minor inconveniences that disrupted the schooners' smooth operations to near disasters that resulted in the loss of life or extensive damage to the vessels. The *Frank A. Palmer* grounded on at least two occasions, once off New Jersey and once at the entrance to Vineyard Sound. In both cases, the schooner was fully loaded and in a perilous situation, but quick action by salvage tugs saved the day.[40]

Sailing year round, the great coal schooners encountered many of the worst Atlantic storms. Loaded to capacity with coal, a schooner had relatively little freeboard when sailing on an even keel. Strong winds and high seas often caused the decks at amidships to be partially awash. The exceedingly long wooden hulls of the great schooners leaked, and foundering in heavy weather was always a possibility. Steam-powered pumps kept the rising water at bay; however, pump malfunctions could doom a schooner that leaked heavily. In February 1901, a storm caught the *Louise B. Crary* on its way to Galveston. The storm washed the first mate overboard, and the large seas caused the schooner to roll on its beam ends for four days.[41]

Collisions were an ever-present danger in the New England coal trade. The great coal schooners' sheer size and limited maneuverability caused problems in busy ports. Further increasing the chance of collision, coal schooners often sailed in proximity to one another, following relatively defined routes from port to port. Damage resulting from collisions varied from minor breakage on either of the vessels to the complete loss of both vessels. The *Frank A. Palmer* ran afoul of several vessels; one such incident occurred in May 1901, when the schooner collided with the British steamship *Gadsby* off Sandy Hook, outside New York Harbor. En route to Portland from Philadelphia, the *Frank A. Palmer* had its port bow stove in and lost its port anchor, impaled in the steamer's deckhouse.[42]

The route from Cape Henry to Maine was filled with unpredictable weather, treacherous shoals and fog-hidden headlands. A high degree of skill, knowledge and intuition was needed by coasting schooner captains to navigate the dangers safely. The myriad hazards faced by the great schooners and their tremendous size reduced the average lifespan of this vessel variety to twelve years. In comparison, the lifespan for other vessels, both sail and steam, was twenty years.[43]

COLLISION!

The coal trade's economic realities that led to competition between schooners set the stage for the *Frank A. Palmer* and *Louise B. Crary*'s demise at the mouth of Massachusetts Bay in 1902. The circumstances that led to their proximity were not unusual; in the winter months, the coal schooner fleet anchored in Vineyard Sound awaiting favorable weather to round Cape Cod. Captain W.J. Lewis Parker captured the scene as the coal schooners charged out of Vineyard Sound:

> *When at last "the break" came these anchorages would ring to the sound of pawls slipping over windlasses and the clank of chain as half a hundred anchors came home. Pungent soft coal smoke and spurts of exhaust steam told of the strain on the donkey boilers as the heavy gaffs climbed aloft, the complaining of blocks gave way to a thunder of canvas as each vessel came about, and then silently, with startling suddenness the fleet was gone past Chatham…It was a race in every sense of the word, for the discharging docks were incapable of handling such onslaught, and it was a case of first home, first tug, and first to be docked, discharged, and ready to make the run back to the coal ports before the market was glutted with collier tonnage seeking charter. There was a real sport of racing in those opulent days, when the owners did not protest too strongly if a sail or two blew away.*[44]

During the first weeks of December 1902, Boston suffered an unusually severe cold snap that dropped temperatures into the single digits and below for days at a time. Accompanying strong winter storms held up the coal fleet in Vineyard Sound, limiting supply. New England's dependence on coal to heat homes, schools and businesses; run railroads; operate factories; and generate electricity created a coal famine that severely disrupted daily life.[45] Demand raised the price of coal by as much as three dollars per ton. Once the weather broke, unloading colliers could expect these prices for only a short while, and each collier that arrived in Boston extended the time subsequently arriving vessels would have to wait before unloading. Captain James E. Rawding of the *Frank A. Palmer* and Captain William H. Potter of the *Louise B. Crary* undoubtedly felt the pressure to rapidly discharge their loads and secure a new charter while shippers were willing to pay premium freight rates because of the high demand.

The *Frank A. Palmer*'s voyage north began on December 4, when it left Newport News with approximately 3,700 tons of coal. Similarly burdened, the *Louise B. Crary* departed Newport News on December 8. While sailing north, bad weather temporarily delayed the *Frank A. Palmer* behind the Delaware Breakwater at Cape Henlopen until December 10. The weather improved enough for the schooner to reach Vineyard Haven, where it joined a large fleet of colliers, including the *Louise B. Crary*, at anchor awaiting calmer weather.

By December 17, both schooners had rounded Cape Cod and were sailing toward Boston using a strong northwest wind. Southeast of Cape Ann, the schooners split tacks and came about on a collision course. The *Louise B. Crary*'s mate, J.E. Smith, had the schooner heading northwest on a port tack while the *Frank A. Palmer*'s mate steered southwest on a starboard

Sonar image of the collided schooners *Frank A. Palmer* and *Louise B. Crary*, still connected more than one hundred years later. *NOAA/SBNMS and Applied Signal Technology.*

tack. In this position, the *Frank A. Palmer* had the right of way. Tragically, Mate Smith did not yield his vessel, believing that he would safely cross the *Frank A. Palmer*'s bow. As a result, the *Louise B. Crary* slammed into the *Frank A. Palmer* portside near its forecastle at around seven o'clock that night. The *Frank A. Palmer*'s foremast immediately fell, and the schooners became tangled in each other's wreckage. Within moments of the collision, both schooners sank beneath the surface, drowning six of the twenty-one sailors involved. Mate J.E. Smith made no attempt to save himself when Captain Potter ordered him to abandon ship. The remaining fifteen men struggled into the *Frank A. Palmer*'s longboat. Racing to save themselves from drowning, most of the men rushed from their bunks without grabbing warm clothing, and none was able to secure food or water.

The survivors now faced a terrible ordeal as they drifted east of Massachusetts Bay in the middle of winter awaiting rescue. Although the longboat was equipped with oars, the bitter cold quickly sapped the survivors' strength, and they were only able to keep the longboat's bow into the waves. Over the next four nights, four crewmen died from exposure while one man experienced hallucinations after drinking seawater and committed suicide by jumping overboard. On the morning of December 21, the fishing schooner *Manhassett* picked up the ten remaining sailors sixty miles southeast of Highland Light, Cape Cod, and brought them into Boston. Several of the frostbitten semiconscious men were taken to the hospital for treatment. Four days later, one of the most injured sailors died from the effects of exposure. In total, only nine of the original twenty-one crewmen made it through the ordeal.[46]

LOCKED IN TIME: THE *FRANK A. PALMER*'S AND *LOUISE B. CRARY*'S ARCHAEOLOGICAL REMAINS

The *Frank A. Palmer* and *Louise B. Crary* shipwreck was introduced to the sanctuary by H. Arnold Carr, who along with his partner, John P. Fish, spent the 1980s surveying the sanctuary's waters to locate the steamship *Portland*. During the countless hours that the men spent mapping the sanctuary's seafloor with sonar, they located numerous other shipwrecks, some of which they shared with sanctuary managers. During the sanctuary's first mission to explore the *Portland* in 2002 with NURC-UConn researchers, the team also surveyed the collided schooners with side-scan sonar. The resulting image amazed all onboard the research cruise; the twin hulls sitting upright on the

The remains of Captain J.E. Rawding's chronometer in the *Frank A. Palmer*'s stern cabin. *NOAA/SBNMS and NURTEC-UConn.*

seafloor joined at their bows perfectly conveyed the vessels' final moments. It was even possible to ascertain which vessel was which. The four-masted *Frank A. Palmer* had three clearly defined cargo hatches, and the five-masted *Louise B. Crary* had four cargo hatches.

Sanctuary archaeologists first explored the shipwreck with a ROV in 2003, with continuing investigations in 2004, 2005 and 2006. Utilizing the NURC-UConn *Hela* ROV, the research team photographed and video documented the shipwrecks, collected geographic positions of identifiable features and noted changes to the site.

The *Frank A. Palmer* and *Louise B. Crary* lie partially embedded in a mud bottom at a depth of 350 feet, twenty miles off Gloucester. The schooners sit upright with their bows in contact near their point of impact. The *Frank A. Palmer*'s port bow appears to be partially crushed beneath the *Louise B. Crary*'s starboard side adjacent to the *Frank A. Palmer*'s foremast. Together, the schooners' hulls form a "V" pointing west.

The *Frank A. Palmer*'s wooden hull has survived from the main deck level down to the keel; however, the schooner is missing its fly rail from atop

Trapped air blew the *Frank A. Palmer*'s aft deckhouse roof free when it sank, allowing a view of the captain's head. *NOAA/SBNMS and NURTEC-UConn.*

its bulwarks. The schooner's stern section, including the transom, helm and steering mechanism, is mostly intact except for a ten-foot section of the port stern quarter beneath the quarter bitts where outer hull planking had eroded away, exposing the tops of the futtocks. The after deckhouse roof is missing, exposing the captain's cabin and head. Portions of the cabinetry and doors that divided the deckhouse are discernable, as are the captain's copper-sheathed ceramic toilet and sink. Smaller artifacts, including bottles, a stoneware jug, dishware, an oil lamp base and a clock, lie on the deckhouse floor.

Side-scan sonar and ROV surveys of the *Louise B. Crary* revealed a substantially intact hull consisting of articulated outer hull planking, frames, inner hull planking, deck planking and deck beams. ROV investigations imaged the bow and bowsprit and the portside bulwarks, including five sets of chain plates. Like the *Frank A. Palmer*, the schooner's fly rail is missing. Amidships, the cargo hatch coamings are intact, with wire rope standing rigging crisscrossing its deck. Portions of the *Louise B. Crary*'s rigging lie off the vessel's portside, including the top of one of its masts with attached trestletrees and blocks. The stern of the schooner is inaccessible to close inspection due to entangled fishing nets; however, portions of the aft deckhouse are visible beneath the nets.

Overall, the appearance of the site was of two schooners that sank intact after their collision. The position of the schooners corroborated historical accounts that the *Frank A. Palmer* sank first and the *Louise B. Crary* shortly afterward, as the *Louise B. Crary* appears to rest partially on top of the *Frank A. Palmer's* port bow. Site preservation is excellent due to the schooners' size, stoutly built hulls and depth of water, which negates most winter wave action. Unfortunately, commercial bottom trawls and gillnets have ensnared portions of the wrecks, breaking pieces from them and hampering the site's complete documentation. In 2006, the National Park Service listed the collided remains of the *Frank A. Palmer* and *Louise B. Crary* on the National Register of Historic Places as the best example of the great New England coal schooners located to date.

THE *PAUL PALMER*: THE UNLUCKY "HOODOO" SCHOONER

Even though Bath produced the most five-masted schooners, Waldoboro, Maine, came to the forefront of five-masted schooner construction in 1900, when William F. Palmer chose the yard of George L. Welt to build 6 schooners for his fleet, known as the "(Second) Palmer Fleet." Originally settled in the early 1700s on the Medomak River, Waldoboro's forest product trade grew into a shipbuilding center. Waldoboro shipyards turned out two- and three-masted schooners as their staple, launching 225 vessels between 1840 and 1860.[47] The shipyards even produced 4 four-masted schooners between 1886 and 1890. Declining shipbuilding orders after 1890 led to a skilled and underutilized workforce, on which William F. Palmer capitalized.

Between 1900 and 1909, William F. Palmer built and managed a fleet of fifteen coal schooners out of Boston—known as the "Great White Fleet," as all had white hulls. His success was truly amazing, as he started with no prior experience in the maritime trades and assumed responsibility for schooner design, management, coordination of activities and financing. Palmer's interest in the coal trade likely germinated while he was headmaster of the Bristol Academy in Taunton, Massachusetts. Taunton, in the 1890s, was a major distribution point for bituminous coal in New England.

At the beginning of the twentieth century, America's coal schooner shares became an investment mechanism used by well-to-do individuals, as opposed to a community-based enterprise, and the management of schooners was increasingly concentrated in fewer hands. A biographical sketch of Palmer related, "Nothing but incessant industry, eternal vigilance and business genius of a high order could have enabled Mr. Palmer not merely to hold his own, but to increase his tonnage so enormously that the Palmer house flag is recognized everywhere between the Bay of Fundy and the Caribbean as that of one of the merchant kings of the Atlantic coast."[48]

William F. Palmer's first vessel, the Bath-built four-masted schooner *Marie Palmer*, paid out a very lucrative 27 percent return to its investors and established Palmer in the business. He returned to the Bath shipyards for his second vessel, *Maude Palmer*, shortly thereafter. Seeking to build a larger schooner, William F. Palmer contracted with shipbuilder George L. Welt in 1899 for the construction of the five-masted schooner *Fannie Palmer*. William F. Palmer was an astute businessman who likely saw an opportunity to use George L. Welt's shipyard as a way to achieve a lower building cost than he could negotiate at Bath.

On May 28, 1901, William F. Palmer and George L. Welt signed a contract for the construction of hull "No. 7," which became the *Paul Palmer*. William F. Palmer agreed to pay the builder a sum of $75,000, with final delivery due on April 10, 1902. George L. Welt's yard laid *Paul Palmer*'s keel in November 1901; however, little work was done until the following spring. Palmer stayed intimately involved in the schooner's construction; not even the smallest details escaped his purview. In particular, he sought to remedy defects in earlier schooners. During the final months of construction, Charles E. Risley, the *Paul Palmer*'s first captain, visited the shipyard frequently to represent Palmer's interests.[49]

On August 19, 1902, the *Paul Palmer* slid down its ways into the Medomak River. Named after William F. Palmer's infant son, the schooner's enrolled dimensions were 276.1 feet in length, 44.2 feet in breadth and a 24.4-foot depth of hold. Its gross and net tonnages were, respectively, 2,193 tons and 1,763 tons.[50] Georgia pine planking, some 675,000 board feet, went into its hull planking and decking; 450 tons of Virginia's best oak created its frames; thirty thousand locust treenails secured the outer hull planking; and 150 tons of iron bolts secured the inner hull planking. Its five masts were all Oregon pine; the main masts were 116.0 feet long, and its topmasts were 60.0 feet long. These masts were likely the *Paul Palmer*'s most expensive components due to their size and the shipment cost from Oregon by rail. Rigging and sails also made up another significant portion of its construction cost. Mechanical assistance allowed the schooner to sail with only a ten-man crew; a twenty-five-horsepower Hyde reversible steam-powered hoisting engine helped to raise and lower the sails, and a steam-powered windlass handled the schooner's two large Baldt stockless anchors.[51]

Glisteningly white on its launching day, the *Paul Palmer*'s upper hull, deckhouses, stanchions, fly rail and bowsprit carried the Great White Fleet's standard paint scheme. Its lower hull from the waterline down to the keel was painted with a dark-colored anti-fouling paint and sheathed in copper-alloy plates. Additional metal sheathing protected the bow and outer hull to the main mast at the light load to prevent damage while sailing through thin ice. Vessel enrollments specified that it had an eagle head, elliptical stern and two decks. The schooner had a "flush-deck" layout characterized by a weather deck that ran unbroken from stem to stern. The forward deckhouse was recessed into the weather deck and surrounded the foremast. It contained the engineer's stateroom, engine room and eight crew berths. Aft of the mainmast, the midship house contained additional crew berths, galley and dining area. The aft deckhouse held the captain's cabin, steward's

A large crowd gathered to watch the schooner *Paul Palmer*'s launch into the Medomak River at Waldoboro. *Maine Maritime Museum, Bath, Maine.*

room, pantry, first and second mates' room, chart room, wardrobes and three guests' rooms.[52]

A correspondent from the *Lincoln County News* toured the *Paul Palmer*'s deckhouses and cabins on its launching day. He reported that the schooner had unusually large oak- and mahogany-trimmed cabins in the aft deckhouse with all of the modern conveniences, including a bathroom with a large porcelain-lined bathtub, porcelain sink and well-stocked medicine cabinet for the ship's doctor. The captain's cabin had antique oak furniture and even a piano. The mates' cabin and three spare staterooms also occupied the aft deckhouse, which measured thirty-seven feet by thirty-three feet. The midship house contained quarters for the second mate and the cook; it also held the galley and mess rooms. The forward deckhouse held the remaining crew's quarters, described as very comfortable and supplied with all the means necessary to have a pleasant time while not on watch.

THE *PAUL PALMER*'S CAREER

The *Paul Palmer*'s first trip took it from Waldoboro to Philadelphia to load coal for Portland under Captain Charles E. Risley. The schooner departed Philadelphia on September 9, 1902, and arrived in Portland three days later. Over the next ten years and nine months, the *Paul Palmer* sailed back and forth between the Chesapeake, Gulf Coast and New England, transporting coal and very occasionally other bulk cargo such as railroad ties and phosphate. Between 1902 and 1909, managing owner William F. Palmer directed the *Paul Palmer* and up to fifteen other schooners. While individually the *Paul Palmer* could carry 3,300 to 3,400 tons of dead-weight cargo, it was with the Palmer fleet's operations as a whole where William F. Palmer made his mark. In 1903, the Great White Fleet was able to transport 35,000 tons of cargo a month. By the beginning of 1904, the schooners could carry up to 42,000 tons a month.[53]

During the *Paul Palmer*'s twelve years of operation, the schooner completed 207 successful transits between ports and loaded approximately eighty coal cargos. While the actual tonnage of each cargo is unknown, an average coal cargo for the *Paul Palmer* weighed 3,500 tons; therefore, the *Paul Palmer* transported an estimated 280,000 tons of coal in its lifetime. The *Paul Palmer* primarily loaded coal cargos at Newport News and less frequently at Baltimore, Philadelphia and Norfolk. These cargos were delivered mostly to the New England cities of Boston, Portsmouth, Bangor, Portland and

The schooner *Paul Palmer* discharging coal at Portsmouth, New Hampshire. *Library of Congress, Detroit Publishing Company Collection, LC-DIG-det-4a18384.*

Providence, while the southern cities of Searsport, Galveston, San Juan, Punta Gorda and Port Tampa received the remainder. In addition to its coal cargos, the *Paul Palmer* carried at least ten phosphate, eight railroad tie, one ice and one sugar cargo(s).[54]

William F. Palmer's death in September 1909 did not lead to the immediate dissolution of his fleet. Instead, one year later, the firm of J.S. Winslow and Company took over the Palmer fleet's management, which consisted of twelve schooners valued at over $1,000,000. At that time, J.S. Winslow and Company managed twenty-two schooners. After the transaction, the company controlled thirty-four schooners, making it the single largest fleet manager. Once under the control of J.S. Winslow and Company, all of the Great White Fleet had their hulls painted black to reflect the management transfer.[55]

Like many of the large coal schooners, the *Paul Palmer* had a variety of mishaps. Historian Ralph D. Paine described the often-overlooked skill needed and hazards faced by the crew of the coastwise shipping trade:

> *To speak of this deep-water shipping as coastwise is misleading. The words convey an impression of dodging from port to port for short distance, whereas many of the voyages are longer than those of the foreign routes in European waters. It is farther by sea from Boston to Philadelphia than from Plymouth, England to Bordeaux...This coastwise trade may lack the romance of the old school square rigged ship in the Roaring Forties, but it has always been more perilous and exacting. Its seamen suffer hardships unknown elsewhere, for they have to endure the winters of intense cold and heavy gales and they are always in the risk of stranding or being driven ashore.*[56]

As the *Paul Palmer* sailed the eastern seaboard, its captain and crew found themselves in shoal water on several occasions that exemplify the variety of places navigated by the deep-draft vessel. The *Paul Palmer* grounded with little injury in April 1903 in the channel off Fort Carroll, near Baltimore, and again in July 1905 in the harbor at Bangor, while docking. Most seriously, the schooner grounded on Tennessee Reef off the Florida Keys during a transit from Newport News to Port Tampa in May 1912. In order to free the vessel, the crew jettisoned two hundred tons of its coal cargo to lessen its draft.[57]

Even though a coal schooner's greatest peril was at sea, there was also a risk to the vessel and crew while sitting in port. The *Paul Palmer*'s first experience with a dockside fire occurred in January 1907, when it nearly caught fire while loading coal at Baltimore's Hamilton Coal Company pier. A tug and fireboat pulled the schooner to safety.[58] The *Paul Palmer*'s next brush with fiery destruction occurred in July 1908 while discharging coal at the Massachusetts Coal Company's dock in East Boston. A large fire erupted at the Grand Junction Docks, quickly engulfing much of the waterfront in an inferno. Tugs managed to pull the schooner out into the harbor as extreme heat and flying debris ignited the schooner's foretopmast. The tugs then extinguished the fire before it spread to the rest of the schooner's rigging.[59]

FIRE!

After unloading a coal cargo in Bangor, Maine, Captain Howard B. Allen turned the *Paul Palmer* south for Newport News. The schooner stopped for a day at Rockport, Maine, and then resumed its trip on Friday, June 13, 1913. Allen anticipated a routine early summer passage and welcomed two passengers onboard: his wife and their friend Miss Catherine Dunn of Dorchester, Massachusetts. Two days later, a fire broke out in the forward deckhouse at three o'clock in the afternoon as the *Paul Palmer* approached Cape Cod. While the fire's specific cause was never determined, it originated in the forecastle, where the ship's most flammable supplies were stored. On June 19, 1913, the *Provincetown Advocate* wrote, "[The fire] gained headway, with marvelous rapidity from the moment of discovery, increasing with such quickness and fury that the pump space in the forward deckhouse was made untenable by the time the fire hose had been coupled on, forcing the crew to flee the flames." Sailing in ballast and therefore riding high in the water, the crew's attempts to fight the fire with buckets was even more difficult and ultimately ineffectual.

Captain Allen turned the *Paul Palmer* toward Cape Cod, raised as much sail as he could muster and hoisted the Stars and Stripes upside down to signal distress. At the same time, the light keeper at Highland Light sighted the burning vessel sixteen miles offshore and put out a call for vessels to help. The Allens, Miss Dunn and the eleven-man crew battled the blaze for three hours to no avail. Help arrived in the form of the tug *Western* and the schooners *Rose Dorothea* and *Vigilant*, along with the steamship *Massachusetts*. The tug's crew used its pumps to drench the fire but had no success. By 6:00 p.m., Captain Allen found the situation to be untenable and had his crew and passengers disembark in the schooner's yawl boat, a difficult task in the heavy seas caused by a strong northeast wind. Captain Allen was the last man to leave. Within moments of the boat's departure, the *Paul Palmer*'s forward two masts fell across its stern quarter. In the meantime, Captain Bragg of the famed fishing schooner *Rose Dorothea* maneuvered his schooner

The schooner *Rose Dorothea*, winner of the 1907 Fisherman's Race, rescued the *Paul Palmer*'s crew as the schooner burned. *Library of Congress, Detroit Publishing Company Collection, LC-DIG-det-4a16000.*

into position and rescued the *Paul Palmer*'s passengers and crew. The fishing schooner transported all onboard into Provincetown, and within an hour the schooner burned to its waterline.[60]

The *Paul Palmer*, still aflame and adrift near the shipping lanes, posed a significant hazard to shipping. The U.S. Revenue Cutter Service dispatched its cutters *Androscoggin* and *Gresham* to search for the wreck and destroy it. When the *Gresham* arrived at the sunken wreck, reported as six miles north by east of Race Point, three of its masts floated above the hull still attached to the rigging. On June 16, 1913, the *Boston Herald* reported on the *Paul Palmer*'s misfortune:

> *While the cause of the fire could not be learned, all the old sailors along the coast were able to account to their own satisfaction for the disaster to the big schooner. She put in at Rockport, Me., on her way down the coast and sailed from that port on Friday the 13th without cargo. The old salts*

wagged their heads and asked, "What do you expect? Friday is bad enough,
Friday the 13th is worse, but when it comes to Friday the 13th, 1913,
something is bound to happen."

Historian Paul Morris catalogued the final dispositions of all fifty-eight East Coast–built five-masted schooners. He found that nineteen were abandoned at sea or foundered; eight were lost due to collision; eight were broken up, condemned or abandoned as useless; four were sold to foreign owners; four were lost due to enemy action during war; one was lost due to grounding; one went missing; and one had an unknown fate. The *Paul Palmer* was the only one to sink at sea as a result of a fire onboard.[61]

THE *PAUL PALMER*'S ARCHAEOLOGICAL REMAINS

The *Paul Palmer* holds archaeological site designation STB001 as the very first shipwreck investigated by Stellwagen Bank sanctuary researchers. First located in 2000 following multi-beam sonar mapping of the sanctuary's seafloor by the U.S. Geological Survey, focused side-scan sonar and SCUBA diving surveys in 2002 determined the shipwreck was the remains of a large wooden-hulled sailing vessel from the late nineteenth to early twentieth centuries. Comparison of the shipwreck's size, orientation, observed site characteristics and location to the historical record indicated that STB001 was the *Paul Palmer*.

Located approximately seven miles north of Cape Cod on Stellwagen Bank's flat sandy seafloor at a depth of eighty feet, the *Paul Palmer* is the sanctuary's shallowest shipwreck. Stellwagen Bank's shifting sands partially cover the hull's charred remains oriented on a northeast-to-southwest axis with its bow located at the northeast end. The *Paul Palmer*'s remaining articulated hull is composed of keelsons, sister keelsons, frames, ceiling planking and outer hull planking, essentially the very bottom of the schooner's hull. Its keel is believed to be present but buried. The vessel's orientation caused the starboard side to be mostly covered with sand from the keelsons out to the turn of the bilge, with only the tips of the starboard frames protruding from the sand to a height of one foot. On the port side, sand has filled the ship's bilge up to the top of its keelson. Copper-alloy sheathing, outer hull planking, frames and bilge ceiling extend between one and four feet above the sand near its bow. The shipwreck's largest nonstructural features are its

The *Paul Palmer*'s portside hull remains project from Stellwagen Bank's sandy seafloor. *Matthew Lawrence, NOAA/SBNMS.*

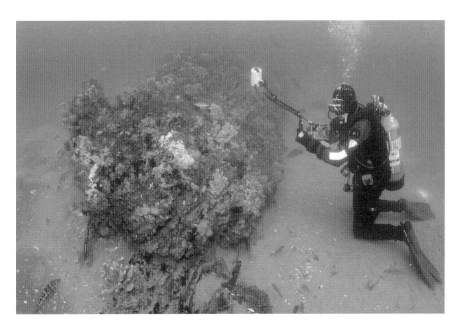

A sanctuary archaeologist photographs the *Paul Palmer*'s stern timbers to record its construction. *Heather Knowles, NADE.*

large steam-powered windlass and studlink anchor chain pile. Other iron fittings found on the wreck include a yawl boat davit, donkey boiler, wire rope, bitts, a topmast step, hoisting machinery and an auxiliary anchor. In total, the shipwreck's articulated remains extend a distance of 260 feet and are 38 feet wide at its greatest breadth. The site's keelsons extend a length of 243 feet and match closely the *Paul Palmer*'s construction contract, which specified a 247-foot-long keel for the schooner. In several places on the forward half of the site, structural timbers such as frames and bilge ceiling are extensively charred. Aside from small bits of coal in the bilge, no other cargo remains were found on the shipwreck. In 2006, the National Park Service listed the *Paul Palmer*'s shipwreck on the National Register of Historic Places due to its involvement in the coal trade.

OTHER STELLWAGEN BANK SANCTUARY COLLIER SHIPWRECKS

Second only to twentieth-century fishing vessel shipwrecks, sunken vessels with coal cargos make up the next most numerous variety of shipwreck located thus far in Stellwagen Bank sanctuary. In addition to the above coal trade–related shipwrecks, archaeological research has located seven

Many other vessels carrying coal cargos sank in the sanctuary, including this small schooner found with a patent taffrail log in its stern cabin. *NOAA/SBNMS and NURTEC-UConn.*

wrecks with coal cargos that have yet to be identified. Historical records indicate that there are potentially an additional eleven vessels sunk in the sanctuary that were carrying coal, primarily schooners and schooner barges that sank during the late nineteenth and early to mid-twentieth centuries. Unfortunately, none is as intact as the *Frank A. Palmer* and *Louise B. Crary*, but each offers different clues about its part in the coal trade. Several of the wrecks have moderate wooden hull preservation and some exceptional artifacts, while others are only coal cargo piles with larger metal items such as anchors and windlasses. Despite the lack of substantial hull remains, the documentation and study of these colliers can still reveal much about waterborne transportation of coal in New England. Ongoing research is attempting to identify the unnamed collier shipwrecks, and future surveys will undoubtedly locate additional coal-laden wrecks.

HISTORICALLY REPORTED COLLIER SHIPWRECKS IN STELLWAGEN BANK SANCTUARY

Name	Vessel Variety	Year Built	Length (Feet)	Year Lost	Cause of Loss	Cargo
Joseph Hall	two-mast schooner	1850	78.4	1888	collision	coal
Jessie L. Leach	two-mast schooner	1863	110	1922	foundered	anthracite coal valued at $3,700
Jennie R. Morse	three-mast schooner	1878	137.8	1886	collision	coal, 800 tons
Yemassee	schooner barge	1879	228.4	1916	foundered	anthracite coal valued $10,000
Modoc	two-mast schooner	1882	99.8	1908	foundered	anthracite coal
Hattie H. Barbour	three-mast schooner	1883	121.5	1917	foundered	coal valued at $2,660
King Philip	four-mast schooner	1886	211	1898	foundered	coal, 1,787 tons
William Johnson	four-mast schooner	1890	174	1898	foundered	coal, 1,200 tons valued at $4,000
Frank A. Palmer	four-mast schooner	1897	274.5	1902	collision	bituminous coal, 3,700 tons

SHIPWRECKS OF STELLWAGEN BANK

Name	Vessel Variety	Year Built	Length (Feet)	Year Lost	Cause of Loss	Cargo
786	schooner barge	1899	141.6	1926	foundered	anthracite coal, 1,101 tons
Louise B. Crary	five-mast schooner	1900	267	1902	collision	bituminous coal, 3,702 tons
Paul Palmer	five-mast schooner	1902	276.1	1913	fire	in ballast
John Tracy	screw steamship	1919	253.4	1927	foundered	coal, 4,000 tons
Sintram	five-mast schooner	1920	266	1921	collision	coal, 3,764 tons valued at $50,000

Sailing Tombstones

Granite from Land to Sea

Granite's Early Use in New England

When the first colonists arrived on the shores of Massachusetts Bay, they found a large supply of exposed granite boulders available for building foundations. Increased population density, particularly in Boston, led to more use of granite in building construction throughout the 1600s, but wooden houses predominated. However, large fires, in particular the 1679 blaze on Boston's waterfront that destroyed many wooden clapboard structures and caused $1 million of damage, emphasized the need for stone construction among closely spaced buildings. No longer able to find sufficient stone in proximity to Boston's core, builders looked outward. The origins of New England's granite quarrying industry can be traced to Quincy, a coastal community ten miles south of Boston. Early quarrying techniques involved heating granite boulders and then smashing them with an iron ball. The fragments were then hammered into the desired shape. Kings Chapel in Boston was the first large building constructed of Quincy granite and one of the first examples of granite's transportation from its original location to a work site. Masons began construction on the chapel in 1749 and completed it in 1754, drawing crowds of visitors to see the marvel.

German immigrants who settled in Quincy introduced better methods to quarry stone. At first, quarrymen used gunpowder to break off large sections of exposed granite that was then hammered into straighter and smoother pieces. By the end of the eighteenth century, Quincy quarrymen adopted a new, more efficient technique known as feather and wedge splitting. Quarrymen using this method carved short, narrow slots along their desired axis of cleavage. Steel wedges driven into the slot between thin iron shims called "feathers" split the granite more precisely. Following the turn of the century, Quincy stonecutters increased their output and lowered their rates by refining quarrying techniques further. Rather than carving slots in the stone, quarrymen drilled a series of round holes six inches apart and then used wedges and feathers to split the rock along the drill holes, producing remarkably angular and uniform pieces.[62]

In 1800, several entrepreneurs opened quarries in Quincy and Braintree, establishing the first stone businesses in the region. At first, demand for large building stones was low due to the high labor cost and difficulty in delivering the stone to the work site. Instead, the quarries concentrated on small building underpinnings and doorsteps.

Plans to commemorate the Battle of Bunker Hill with a monument sparked a revolution in Quincy's granite industry in the 1820s. The Bunker Hill Monument Association commissioned architect Solomon Willard to build his winning design for a 221-foot-high granite obelisk. Willard sought out quarries to deliver the stone, and after finding none suitable, he took on the challenge himself, choosing a four-acre property in Quincy that became the Bunker Hill Quarry. Most remarkably, he then invented the machinery to move the three-and-a-half-ton slabs with the United States' first commercial railway. Chains and counterbalanced weights lowered loaded stone cars down steep inclines and returned empty cars to the quarry face. On shallower pitches, ox or horsepower moved the stone from the quarry to the company's wharf on the Neponset River near Gulliver's Creek for shipment to Charlestown. Around the same time, the Quincy Canal Corporation extended the head of the Town River to within a mile of several quarries, enabling sloops to load granite cargos brought down by wagon. Solomon Willard's operations dropped delivered stone costs by almost fivefold, stimulating New England's granite industry and highlighting granite's use as a monumental building material.[63]

Between 1803 and 1847, twenty-eight firms engaged in the granite business with hundreds of men per year employed in the trade that earned Quincy its nickname, "Granite City." In the following years, Quincy granite made it into many landmark buildings, such as the United States Customhouses in Boston, Savannah, New Orleans and Galveston. In the 1870s, Quincy began shifting away from waterborne transportation, as regional railroads connected with the local quarry rail lines. Around the

A granite-carrying sloop arrives at the Charlestown Navy Yard in 1833, joining a topsail schooner already discharging its stone cargo. *Library of Congress, LC-DIG-pga-00196.*

same time, Quincy quarries changed their output to cutting and dressing granite for monumental and ornamental work. Mechanized quarries used large turning mills to produce columns, and stonecutters with air-powered tools fashioned ornate pieces of art from highly polished gray-, green- and pink-colored granite.[64]

CAPE ANN QUARRIES EXPAND THE GRANITE TRADE

Quincy's rapidly developing granite industry and advances in quarrying techniques led to the industry's expansion at Cape Ann, a rocky island promontory north of Boston. Cape Ann's exposed, almost inexhaustible granite outcrops close to the ocean made it an ideal quarry location. The quarries formed an almost continuous line along the coast from Rockport to Bay View. Until 1800, Cape Ann granite was used locally for foundations, mooring stones, millstones, street markers and well curbing.[65] In 1823, Mr. Nehemiah Knowlton cut five hundred tons of cobble near Pigeon Cove and shipped it into Boston on the thirty- to forty-ton sloop *Fox*, marking the first time that city received Cape Ann stone. Early uses of the granite included government fortification work on the Boston Harbor Islands, the naval shipyards in Charlestown and Portsmouth, Salem's jail and Newburyport's customhouse during the 1840s and 1850s.[66]

Aside from these local monumental building projects, Cape Ann granite reached San Francisco, New Orleans and Valparaiso, Chile.[67] Until the end of the Civil War, individually owned operations supplied most of Cape Ann's granite. However, the later decades of the nineteenth century saw William Torrey, Ezra Eames, Amos Sanborn and Beniah Colburn combining their holdings and forming larger companies such as the Bay

Cape Ann's quarries created massive openings in the rocky headland as its stone built America's cities. *Library of Congress, Detroit Publishing Company Collection, LC-DIG-det-4a22615.*

State Granite Company; Gloucester and Boston Granite Company; and Eames, Stimson and Company.

Cape Ann granite's coarse nature made it ideally suited for paving blocks. John Stimson cut some of the area's first pavers from the Flat Ledge Quarry during the 1830s and sent the load to Fort Warren on the sloop *Fox*. Cape Ann quarries pioneered new paving block varieties, in particular the New York block, which was the first type to be laid on its edge. The consolidated quarries produced tremendous quantities of paving blocks, exemplified by a 5.5-million-block order that the Cape Ann Granite Company took on for Boston's streets in 1874. Similar large paving contracts were shipped out on three-masted schooners averaging two-hundred-ton burden to Philadelphia, Baltimore, New York and Washington, D.C. By 1899, most of the larger U.S. cities were using granite street pavers; New York led the nation with 2.64 square miles paved, followed by Philadelphia and Boston, a distant third. Over a twelve-year period between 1918 and 1929, the Rockport Granite Company produced 33,240,947 paving blocks shipped out on schooners.[68]

THE STONE SLOOP'S DEVELOPMENT AND USE

Cape Ann granite quarries utilized a variety of vessels depending on the cargos' size, variety and final destination. While the quarries chartered vessels from the general coasting trade, many owned more specialized vessels ideally suited to the task. In particular, the Cape Ann quarries relied on small sloops, known as "stone sloops," which were ideally suited to shipping cargos of wharf and breakwater granite, cellar stone or building stone because of their heavy construction, lifting derrick and good sailing qualities with heavy loads. Historical records indicate that at least ninety sloops, ranging from forty-five to one hundred feet in length, engaged in the stone trade during the nineteenth and early twentieth centuries. Maine and Massachusetts shipyards built both keel and centerboard vessels, with Freeport, Harpswell and Yarmouth turning out a majority of the fleet.[69]

Published sources attributed the first purpose-built stone sloop to the Pigeon Hill Granite Company's *Ann Parker*, launched in 1850, followed by the *Daniel Webster* (forty-six tons) in 1853. The Rockport Granite Company built its own vessels, *Cock of the Walk* (fifty-five tons) and *New Era* (sixty-two tons), around the same time. A succession of vessels followed over the following decades, each generally growing in size. Notable vessels included the Lanesville Granite Company's *Hard Chance* (sixty-four tons), launched in Gloucester in 1859, and the Rockport Granite Company's *Belle of Cape Ann* (seventy-eight tons), launched in Chatham, Connecticut, in 1860. All of the previously mentioned vessels were keel vessels. Centerboard sloops first appeared with the *C.E. Trumbull* (ninety-nine tons), built in East Boston in 1870, and remained a popular option, exemplified by the *Mary A. White*, built in Boston in 1893.[70]

Cape Ann's stone sloops had a single fore- and aft-rigged mast. A sloop's sail plan included a main sail, jumbo or forestaysail, one or two jibs and a gaff topsail. The sloops were heavily timbered (especially the deck and deck beams), with a broader beam as compared to other contemporary sloops. Stone sloops generally had sharp lines with clipper-type bows and a raised quarterdeck that housed the captain and crew; however, Quincy's quarries favored a more scow-like hull. The crew consisted of a captain, cook and three or four deckhands who helped with loading, sailing and unloading.

Stone sloops used a removable derrick to lift the granite on and off the vessel. When needed, the derrick was stepped just aft of the main mast into a large pillow block; otherwise, it was stowed flat on deck. Block and tackle connected to a hoisting winch made it possible to lift and lower the cargo. In 1851, the sloop *John Brooks* was the first vessel equipped with a steam-hoisting engine, followed by the sloops *New Era* and *Hard Chance* in 1858 and 1859, respectively. Prior to the installation of steam engines, sailors lifted the granite onboard with the sloop's windlass operated by pump brakes or handspikes.[71]

Granite stowage was a precise balancing act carefully attended by the vessel's master. Stowage of large granite pieces in a vessel's hold was limited by the inability to move the granite once it was away from the hatch. Therefore, large-dimension stone was frequently secured on deck once sufficient granite was stowed below to ballast the vessel. Historic photographs depict granite sloops with decks full of cut granite slabs positioned like a jigsaw puzzle surrounding the cargo hatch. Smaller granite pieces like street pavers were always carried below decks, as their potential to shift was high.[72]

MAINE QUARRIES BECOME INDUSTRY LEADERS

Maine became a center of the granite industry in New England after the American Civil War. Past glaciation exposed much of the state's granite underpinnings, and its granite headlands and islands offered easy access to both

A schooner loading large granite slabs at the John L. Goss quarry in Stonington, Maine, around 1900. *Maine Maritime Museum, Bath, Maine.*

the stone and the sea. Its competitive advantage lay with its access to tidewater and the ability to quarry exposed granite without needing to excavate large pits, as was done at the Cape Ann and Quincy quarries. At many places, vessels of over 150 tons could dock a few hundred feet from where the stone was quarried.[73] With the exception of a few quarries located in Oxford, Cumberland, Somerset, Waldo and Hancock Counties, all of Maine's granite quarries were adjacent to or within four miles of navigable tidewater. Maine's best-known granite quarries were at Jonesboro, Vinalhaven, Mount Desert Island and Deer Isle/Stonington. In the 1880s, the largest operations were on Dix, Hurricane, Fox and Crotch Islands. Stone for the New York Customhouse, New York Post Office and Philadelphia Post Office came from Dix Island.[74]

Hurricane Island had its peak quarry years between 1870 and 1900. David Tilson owned the first quarry operations on that island, and in 1870, he and William C. Kingsley formed the Hurricane Island Granite Company, which supplied the stone for the St. Louis Post Office and Customhouse. Built between 1873 and 1884, the stone cutting alone cost the U.S. government $1.47 million. Following several mergers, Hurricane Island quarries cut stone until 1916, when all quarrying on the island ceased.

Lying east of Dix Island at the mouth of West Penobscot Bay, the Fox Islands played an important role in Maine's granite industry. Vinalhaven

Island, the largest island in the group, had its quarry operations concentrated around the town of Vinalhaven and adjacent Carver's Harbor. Both towns had protected harbors with good water access to the island's signature gray and bluish gray stone. Granite quarrying on Vinalhaven Island likely started in the 1820s, with the first granite cargo shipped on the schooner *Plymouth Rock* for the Massachusetts State Prison in Charlestown.[75]

In 1853, the firm of Bodwell, Webster and Company changed the granite business at Vinalhaven, securing large government contracts to supply granite for breakwaters, lighthouses and fortifications. By 1871, the incorporated Bodwell Granite Company produced stone for the Executive Office Building in Washington, D.C.; the Chicago Board of Trade; the Pennsylvania Railroad Station; and the Brooklyn Bridge. Monumental building contracts flowed to the firm between 1880 and 1910, with Vinalhaven stone going into the U.S. Customhouse in New York; post offices in Washington, Pittsburgh, Cincinnati and Kansas City; and the Brooklyn Bridge. The Bodwell Granite Company also owned a fleet of schooners to move the firm's stone; furthermore, its quarries were ideally located for ease of transportation. A system of graded tracks and rail cars moved the stone at most one thousand feet from the quarry face to the loading piers. In 1919, the Bodwell Granite Company closed and sold off all its assets, but smaller companies quarried paving blocks on Vinalhaven Island until 1939.[76]

The southern tip of Deer Isle, and in particular the town of Stonington, was a nexus for Maine's granite industry. Around 1860, Job Goss started working an ideal outcropping at Green's Landing (incorporated as Stonington in 1897). His son, John L. Goss, expanded operations onto Crotch Island and Moose Island just offshore. Due to Crotch Island's easily accessible granite and surrounding deep water, it hosted three active quarries by 1905. The John L. Goss Corporation supplied Crotch Island granite for the Pilgrim Monument in Provincetown, Massachusetts; Portsmouth's U.S. Navy drydock; the Cape Cod Canal; and Boston's Museum of Fine Arts.

While not a quarry location, Chebeague Island in Casco Bay played an important role in granite transportation. Located ten miles from Portland, the small island had a long maritime tradition focused on stone sloops. Author William Hauk identified fifty-nine sloops associated with the island, where nearly all male residents worked on a stone sloop at one time or another. Chebeague Island sloops carried quarried ballast stone to shipyards around Casco Bay as early as the 1760s. By the 1830s, the expanding stone fleet had delivered granite for harbor projects all over New England. Chebeague stone sloops carried cut stone and grout (the oddly shaped pieces of granite

Granite quarried at Crotch Island off Stonington had a short trip from the quarry face to an awaiting schooner. *Maine Granite Industry Historical Society*.

A stone sloop offloading granite for a breakwater. *Maine Maritime Museum, Bath, Maine*.

created during quarrying that were not further finished, equivalent to rubble) for breakwaters and/or wharves along Maine's coast from Eastport to Portland, as well as Massachusetts breakwaters at Newburyport, Rockport and Hyannis and wharves in Boston and Fall River. Stone sloops were ideally suited to breakwater work; the vessels could unload the stone into the water using its derrick. Once the stone was raised from the sloop's deck and swung abeam of the vessel, the sloop's captain tripped the dogs, dropping the granite into the water. Dropping stones weighing between six and ten tons caused the sloop to roll wildly, creating havoc on deck.[77]

SCHOONERS REACH NEW PORTS

By the 1870s, two- and three-masted schooners had replaced the stone sloops as the primary carrier of granite to expanding markets beyond New England. The schooner's larger size and cargo-carrying capacity won out; however, a general cargo schooner had to be reconfigured to make it suitable for the stone trade. In addition to strengthening the deck and hull, the schooner's mainmast was moved as far astern as possible to allow a derrick boom stepped against the foremast to swing stone onboard.[78]

Throughout the 1890s and 1900s, granite shipments down the eastern seaboard returned good profits; schooners left Maine for more southerly ports, offloaded their cargo and then picked up a return cargo. Rarely did a schooner engaged in hauling stone return immediately in ballast to the quarry for another load. Many hauled granite from Maine to New Orleans and then sailed in ballast to Pensacola, Florida, to load pine. Others sailed to Baltimore or Philadelphia and then loaded coal before returning to Maine. Other common cargos included lime, coal, salt, pig iron, phosphate, plaster, bricks, cement, dyewood, sand, lumber, ice, corn, oats, wheat, railroad iron, copper ore, fruit, sugar, cooperage, guano and molasses.

Schooners, like the two-masted, 122-foot-long *Annie and Reuben* built in 1891, were often so fully loaded that they were just shy of sinking. Author John F. Leavitt described the results of this practice in his book *Wake of the Coasters*:

> *I have seen the* Annie and Reuben *with something over 200 tons of stone aboard, lying at Crotch Island wharf with the water flowing through the scuppers to the height of an inch or more on the main hatch coaming over the deck. This is in a flat calm. Loaded in such a fashion, the schooners*

*resembled half-tide ledges when at sea, and it is sure the hatches were well
battened down and pumps going steadily the entire trip.*

Built in Bath for the general coasting trade, the *Annie and Reuben* was
later refitted for the stone trade. In comparison, Essex's Tarr and James
shipyard built the ninety-six-foot-long, two-masted schooner *George R.
Bradford* specifically for the stone trade in 1895. Modeled after the stone
sloop *Albert Baldwin*, Tarr and James revised its design by lengthening its
hull and adding a mast. As these schooners went into service, waterborne
granite transportation methods began to shift. By the early 1910s, Maine
quarries moved toward towed barges for large stone orders. The barges
were capable of carrying 1,300 tons of stone, double the quantity
carried by even three-masted schooners. Most importantly, the barges
were easier to load and unload, greatly decreasing stone handling costs
particularly when transporting stone to established cargo terminals with
shore-based derricks.[79]

DECLINE OF THE GRANITE INDUSTRY

Shipbuilder Lyman Pushee of Dennysville, Maine, built the last schooner,
the two-masted, 102-foot-long *Anna Sophia*, for the granite trade in 1923.
Seven years later, the two-masted schooner *M.M. Hamilton* carried granite to
Boston on the last trip made by a Chebeague Island vessel. By 1930, New
England's granite industry was in severe decline, brought about by the use
of cheaper construction materials for buildings and streets. Where granite
once dominated, it was now relegated to use as veneer for concrete and steel
buildings. Granite's weight made it impracticable for buildings greater than
six stories tall.[80] Likewise, asphalt and concrete supplanted granite in road
construction. The preeminent historian of Maine's granite industry, Roger
Grindle, wrote this about the granite trade's sunset:

> *The demise of the industry in the State* [Maine], *and other parts of
> the country as well, has been variously attributed to changing architectural
> styles; alternate building, monument, and paving materials; rising labor
> costs, transportation and technological changes; the no-cemetery movement;
> cut-throat competition among manufacturers; or, simple lack of foresight.*[81]

During the Great Depression, the quarries did not benefit from government spending. A 1935 study by the John L. Goss Company revealed that only 18 of 234 government building contracts included granite as one of the materials. A Bureau of Labor and Statistics report published the same year indicated that employment in the granite industry was only 29 percent of its 1923–25 average. The late 1930s saw a small uptick in business relating to bridge and building expansion, but World War II depressed the industry to its lowest levels, as it severely restricted government building projects and monopolized labor and coal. In the following years after the war, the economic advantage held by Massachusetts' and Maine's quarries ended when strikes, lockouts and poor labor relations allowed the limestone industry to gain political and lobbying power. Politicians secured government contracts for limestone-producing states, such as Indiana, as new bids came due, shutting out the granite industry. Maine's quarries also found that one of their previously great assets—easy tidewater access—became a hindrance, as transportation by rail and truck was cheaper than by water. Landlocked quarries in places such as Barre, Vermont, prospered since they were closer to rail lines and transportation hubs.[82]

An 1894 edition of the illustrated magazine *Stone* expressed the following opinion on granite's position in America's architecture: "Granite is pre-eminently the finest building material in existence…it presents such an imposing view of massiveness and splendor that it is out of sight compared to any building material known for palaces or pantheons."[83] America's distinctive architecture from the nineteenth and early twentieth centuries was due to granite; however, few who pass by a majestic edifice today recognize the labor and skill needed to shape and move the stone from its humble beginnings.

GRANITE TRADE SHIPWRECKS

Shipping granite by water was a hazardous proposition for the sailors involved. The cargo's sheer weight meant that a leak or shifting cargo during a storm could easily cause the vessel's loss. The United States Life-Saving Service reported that there were a total of 592 disasters between 1876 and 1913 on the Atlantic and Gulf Coasts for vessels carrying a cargo of stone or brick (as reports from six years during that time frame were unavailable for analysis, the total number of disasters in that time frame was likely higher). The average number of disasters was 19 per year, with the year 1894 having the greatest number of disasters at 37. A thorough but not exhaustive search of historic newspapers uncovered at least 110 vessels, mostly two-masted schooners, that sank with a granite cargo off New England's shores between 1812 and 1928.[84] Most vessel losses resulted from either a dramatic cargo shift, causing the vessel to capsize, or catastrophic flooding from hull failure, causing the vessel to founder. Vessels that went ashore or rested in shallow water were often salvaged; those that sank in deeper water became a total loss.

Granite trade research yielded a relatively short list of eight historically reported vessel losses that might have occurred in the Stellwagen Bank sanctuary. However, determining conclusively whether the suspect vessels now rest on the sanctuary's seafloor is challenging. As all the potential wrecks foundered offshore, historically reported positions were imprecise or simply unknown. Furthermore, several vessels sank in storms with the loss of all hands, leaving no one to tell the tale. Given the perilous nature of granite cargos, more vessels beyond the eight identified here are expected to have sunk in the sanctuary.

HISTORICALLY REPORTED GRANITE VESSEL SHIPWRECKS IN STELLWAGEN BANK SANCTUARY

Name	Vessel Variety	Year Built	Length (Feet)	Year Lost	Cargo
Lamartine	two-mast schooner	1848	79	1893	cut granite
Lucy D.	three-mast schooner	1866	110	1886	pavers
A. Heaton	three-mast schooner	1868	130.5	1895	pavers
Screamer	sloop	1872	68	1904	cut granite
Edwin I. Morrison	three-mast schooner	1873	137.8	1894	pavers
Addie E. Snow	two-mast schooner	1876	95.8	1898	pavers
Belle Wooster	three-mast schooner	1878	129.2	1902	cut granite
William C. Tanner	four-mast schooner	1890	191.4	1909	granite rubble

Stellwagen Bank sanctuary archaeologists have located four sunken vessels with granite cargos; all lie in the northern half of the sanctuary at depths from 200 to 350 feet. The two deepest sites lie in the sanctuary's muddy basins; shipwreck STB011 is in Tillies Basin, and shipwreck STB032 is in Stellwagen Basin. Shallower sites STB038 and STB042 are on Gloucester Bank and Stellwagen Bank, respectively. These four shipwrecks represent three broad varieties of granite cargos; STB032 and STB042 carried large rectangular granite block/slabs, STB038 carried pavers and STB011 carried precisely cut stone. Identifying the vessels has been a slow process; however, comparing the sanctuary's historical record to archaeological site characteristics has yielded stories of this important and dangerous trade that wrested value from New England's bedrock.

Archaeologists located shipwreck STB011 in 2004 with side-scan sonar. At first, the sonar target was attributed to a rocky outcropping or glacially deposited rock pile, but further reflection suggested that any object with a reflective return on the muddy seafloor was worth investigating. Following the sonar survey, sanctuary archaeologists and NURC-UConn scientists and technicians documented STB011 with an ROV equipped with still and video cameras during several dives in 2004 and 2006. STB011's overall remains measured ninety-three feet long oriented on a northeast-southwest axis by thirty-three feet wide with five feet of vertical relief above the sediment. The site's main feature, its granite cargo pile, was fifty-two feet long by twenty-four feet wide. Little of the vessel's wooden hull was visible, as only small portions of its lower hull planking and frames projected above the sediment around the granite cargo. The articulated hull material, held together with copper-alloy drift bolts and treenails, and the tightly confined cargo pile indicated that significantly more of the vessel's lower hull was buried in the sediment under the granite blocks. The survey found a fragment of the shipwreck's bow surrounding an iron hawse pipe that once guided the vessel's anchor chain at the shipwreck's northeast end.

Repeated ROV transects across the site revealed evidence of sailing vessel rigging, including a wooden double sheave block. An iron fitting believed to be either a mast cap or cap iron—both were used similarly to join spars—lay on the seafloor along with several four-square-foot sections of what appeared to be canvas sailcloth. Two white ceramic plates, one whole and one fragmented, without identifiable markings were found at the site's southwestern end. Most surprisingly, a three-foot-long section of plaid fabric with blue, green and yellow stripes was observed on the cargo pile's edge.

At the heart of the shipwreck, archaeologists counted more than forty large, angular granite slabs. Most had holes bored through the slab's center. Some slabs were rectangular in shape, measuring four to five feet on a side. Others were more intricately shaped, resembling a slice of bread baked in a loaf pan with rebates carved from three sides. A lesser number of one-foot-wide by four-feet-long slabs were intermixed with the larger pieces. Sediment partly obscured numerous additional granite slabs underneath the visible pieces. While on site, the research team was unable to identify the purpose of the granite slabs, but archival research after the cruise revealed them to be sewer catch basin heads.

As city population densities increased during the nineteenth century, public works engineers sought better ways to handle the effluent created by thousands of horses and masses of people. Recognition of the public health issues created by standing sewage led to a system of street and sidewalk construction that funneled waste and storm water from the streets into the city's sewers. STB011's basin heads provided the sidewalk-level covers for the sewer basins installed at street corners. Stonecutters even removed a notch from the basin head's underside at the street corner's apex to allow gutter water to run off from the street into the catch basin and thence into the sewer. Sewer basin heads required a round manhole to allow access into the catch basin to clear debris. A lip cut around the manhole held a manhole cover flush with the sidewalk. Some of the basin heads were further refined with notches on either side to accept street curbing.

STB011's cargo was stacked more than three layers deep, with some slabs laid flat while others were stacked on edge. The wrecking event or post depositional forces may have moved some of the pieces from their original stowed position; however, the tightly confined hull-shaped pile suggested little movement after the vessel sank. Each basin head measured approximately six feet long by five feet wide by one foot thick. The manhole in the basin head's center was 19.2 inches in diameter. Several of the basin heads that lacked a manhole were equally as long but were only three feet wide and closer to 8.0 inches thick.

Overall, the survey determined STB011 to be a small nineteenth-century wooden-hulled sailing vessel carrying a cargo of granite sewer basin heads and a lesser number of other cut granite forms. Cold Gulf of Maine water surrounded the site, resulting in decreased biologic and chemical deterioration of the shipwreck's structure; however, few highly durable ship fittings—such as anchors, rigging and pumps—were found. The side-scan sonar survey that located the shipwreck revealed some scattered material away from the wreck but, more tellingly, a high density of trawl marks.

The schooner *Lamartine*'s granite sewer basin cover cargo was key to determining its identity. *NOAA/SBNMS and NURTEC-UConn.*

These linear furrows in the soft muddy seafloor resulted from trawl doors or associated bottom trawl fishing gear dragging on the seafloor and provided evidence of fishing activity in the area. Advert or inadvertent trawling of the shipwreck likely contributed to the diminished amount of hull structure found above the sediment line; furthermore, the paucity of durable iron artifacts suggested removal of these fittings by bottom trawling. Sections of chain, rope, trawl net and gill net made from synthetic material provided evidence of the shipwreck's disturbance by fishing activity.

While the granite basin covers seemed like a highly diagnostic clue to the shipwreck's identity, review of the sanctuary's historically reported vessel losses did not reveal a likely shipwreck. Fortunately, local maritime researcher Paul F. McCarthy stepped in to help Stellwagen Bank sanctuary's staff search for this wreck's identity. Through his tireless efforts over nearly a five-year period, Mr. McCarthy finally located a newspaper report describing the schooner *Lamartine*'s loss eighteen miles east-southeast of Cape Ann. More importantly, the *Boston Globe* story described the schooner's cargo as "cut stone"—i.e., granite—that had been specifically shaped as opposed to pavers or rough stone. The shipwreck's location east-southeast from Gloucester, matched closely the *Lamartine*'s historically reported loss location. Following this vessel's trail led to the John L. Goss Corporation records held in the Special Collections of the Fogler Library at the University of Maine and ultimately a much more complete story.

THE *LAMARTINE*'S HISTORY

Captain George Washington Thorndike of Camden, Maine, had the Carleton, Norwood and Company shipyard build the two-masted topsail schooner *Lamartine*. When it slid into the ocean off Goose River in August 1848, it measured 79.9 feet long and 22.4 feet wide and had an 8.1-foot depth of hold. Official enrollment documents described the schooner as having one deck, a half poop, a billet head and a square stern.[85] In addition to the *Lamartine*, William Carleton family's shipbuilding business built seventeen barks, thirteen ships, thirteen schooners, ten brigs and two barkentines. Carleton, Norwood and Company was the largest shipbuilder in Camden and also engaged in the sale and transport of coal, lumber, lime, hay and cooperage.[86] The *Lamartine*'s namesake was Alphonse de Lamartine, a French writer, poet and politician considered to be the first French romantic poet.

After the *Lamartine*'s launch, Captain Thorndike took it on voyages from New York to Charleston, South Carolina, and Jacksonville, Florida, and returned with cargos of timber and logwood, a material used in dyes. The schooner also made passages between New York and Franklin, Louisiana; Portland, Maine; and Cuba with unknown cargos. Reports on two of the *Lamartine*'s voyages provided a more detailed glimpse into its activities. On November 7, 1852, the schooner left New York City with a group of sixteen men from Gardiner, Maine, outfitted with diving gear to salvage the shipwreck of the sixty-four-gun Spanish warship *San Pedro de Alcantara*. The warship sank in a fiery explosion off Venezuela in 1815, reportedly carrying $9 million in specie. Bound for Margarita Island, the *Lamartine* hauled the salvage party's equipment, including a steam engine, air pumps, a diving machine, diving bells and submarine armor. The salvage party returned to Maine in July 1853 with a large quantity of treasure and artifacts, including a gold doubloon, silver dollars, a cannon, rigging components and muskets.[87]

A year later, while sailing from Mobile, Alabama, to Cardenas, Cuba, a Spanish brig-of-war fired on but did not hit the *Lamartine* in international waters. Captain Thorndike reported the hostile act to the U.S. consulate in Cuba and was then accused by Spanish authorities of exaggerating the incident. This exchange fell within the much larger political context of tense Spanish-American relations resulting from the Ostend Manifesto, which sought to justify Cuba's acquisition from Spain. Proslavery forces wanted to bring Cuba into the Union as a slave state to maintain a balance of free and slave states in Congress. Ultimately, international outcry forced President Franklin Pierce to denounce the manifesto and table his plans for U.S. expansion directed at satisfying southern interests.[88]

In April 1860, John S. Emery and Company of Boston purchased the *Lamartine*. At that time, the firm held an ownership stake in over seventy-five vessels that carried freight to the West Indies, South America and Europe and in the U.S. coasting trade. John S. Emery and Company was the schooner's managing owner until 1879. While under the command of Captain George S. Grant, the *Lamartine* made numerous trips between Boston, New York and Philadelphia and the smaller Maine towns of Elizabethport, Calais and Sullivan, hauling lumber into the big cities. Aside from Captain Grant, the *Lamartine*'s masters included Joseph A. Graffam and Captains Goldthwaite, Griggs and Salisbury up to 1870. Captains Dowe, J. Abbott, Griggs, Leland, Allen and Barber commanded the vessel for the decade between 1870 and 1880.[89]

In 1880, commission merchant Joseph P. Ellicott of Boston took over the schooner's management, followed in 1881 by Sylvanus G. Haskell, a Deer Isle, Maine merchant and trial justice involved in the lumber and coal trades. During the first half of the decade, infrequent reports of the *Lamartine*'s activities were limited to lumber trips between Bangor and New York City under Captains William E. Gray, J.D. Torrey and Gordon. Ultimately, S.G. Haskell placed the schooner under the command of Captain Eben W. Eaton, also from Deer Isle, in 1890.[90] Research identified six trips between New York City; Portsmouth, New Hampshire; Hoboken; South Amboy; Deer Isle; and Rockport, Massachusetts, with Eaton as master. While likely engaged in the granite trade at some previous point, the *Lamartine*'s first identified granite trip occurred in September 1892 between Deer Isle and New York City.[91]

The University of Maine's Fogler Library holds a collection of John L. Goss Corporation ledgers detailing that organization's quarrying operations. Fortuitously, one of the few extant account books that described the outgoing cargos recorded the *Lamartine*'s two final voyages. Its second-to-last trip departed Deer Isle with granite on April 15, 1893. The schooner's hold and decks held sixty-five pieces of cut granite ranging from three feet to seven feet in length, weighing approximately 131 tons. The granite was cut from four separate quarries: Crotch Island, Allen, Clegg and Goss and Small. New York City stonecutter J. F. Dolan purchased the cargo for delivery to his finishing yard, where he produced stonework for construction projects all over the country and particularly in Savannah. Once unloaded, the *Lamartine* returned to Deer Isle.[92]

Upon reaching its homeport, the *Lamartine*'s crew spent the first part of May loading its next cut granite cargo. The schooner departed on its final voyage from Green's Landing on May 15. It carried a cargo described as eighty-one setts of basin heads from the T. Snow and Company quarry consigned to the Booth Brothers and Hurricane Isle Granite Company of New York. The John L. Goss Corporation acted as the prime contractor on the order, subcontracting the T. Snow and Company quarry (located in Green's Landing) to actually cut the stone valued between twenty-five and twenty-eight dollars a unit.[93]

When the *Lamartine* departed Stonington on Monday, May 15, 1893, the captain's brother, Jeremiah W. Eaton, and cook Myron Powers filled out the crew roster. All hailed from Deer Isle. The schooner encountered moderate weather until the evening of May 16, when winds began to blow heavily from the southeast. Following interviews with the Eatons, the *Gloucester Daily Times* of May 18, 1893, reported the events that led to the schooner's sinking: "About midnight the vessel hove to, making good weather until 3 o'clock Wednesday morning, when she was boarded by a sea and thrown down." After surviving the boarding sea, the *Lamartine*'s crew found that its cargo had shifted, causing it to be unmanageable. The crew tried to right the vessel, but the granite basin heads were too heavy to move, and then the schooner began to leak. The two crewmen manned the pumps while Captain Eaton tried to turn the *Lamartine* for Gloucester Harbor. The *Gloucester Daily Times* reporter described the life and death struggle onboard the schooner:

> *She began to sink rapidly, being on her beam ends, the masts and sails touching the water and lying flat. The captain at the wheel was half submerged in water. Seeing that it would be a question of a very short time when the craft would go down, the captain gave the order to cut away the longboat which hung at the davits.*

Myron Powers stepped in and severed the tackle on one side but was washed overboard and drowned before he made it to the other davit. Captain Eaton attempted to cut the second now submerged davit falls, but he also fell overboard as the *Lamartine* lurched and sank further. He swam back to the schooner, but finding it submerged, he managed to grab the upside-down longboat that had broken free as the schooner sank. Meanwhile, Jeremiah Eaton, who had been manning the pumps forward, ran aft as the schooner sank and hung on to the longboat davits until the schooner was under water. He then swam to his brother, and they struggled to stay afloat as waves kept knocking the men off the overturned boat.

Returning from a trip to Banquero Bank, Captain John McInnis of the fishing schooner *Edith M. McInnis* sighted the *Lamartine* at around seven o'clock in the morning lying low in the water and flying a distress flag twenty miles southeast of Thacher Island. The *Edith M. McInnis* raced toward the *Lamartine*, finally picking up the nearly drowned men in a dory almost a half hour after the distressed schooner sank. When the *Edith M. McInnis* reached Gloucester that afternoon, Captain McInnis expressed to the *Gloucester Times* reporter a feeling of divine intervention that had placed him on the scene in time to save the brothers.[94]

The granite basin heads that proved disastrous for the *Lamartine* were a specialized product of Maine's quarries for a few short decades during the late nineteenth and early twentieth centuries in response to infrastructure expansion and modernization in America's large cities. It's likely that the *Lamartine*'s cargo was intended for one of New York City's boroughs, where sewer network improvements were underway in 1893. During that year, work crews installed seven miles of sewers and culverts, including sixty-seven receiving basins. By 1910, cheaper concrete or iron basin heads replaced the solid granite, and within five years, city engineers incorporated the sewer basin heads into the concrete sidewalk.[95] In 2012, the *Lamartine* was listed on the National Register of Historic Places. Its shipwreck is a physical link to earlier generations who moved the stone and whose hands chiseled the granite blocks that built our great American cities. The *Lamartine*'s cargo of cut granite reveals fascinating details about how granite quarried in New England met the demands of an increasingly urban nation.

ARCHAEOLOGICAL INVESTIGATION OF SHIPWRECK STB038

Initially located with side-scan sonar in June 2009 after following up a reported fishing net hang, archaeologists determined that the sonar target near the fisherman's hang was a pile of durable cargo, possibly bricks. Site investigations with ROVs revealed a large mound of granite pavers and earned the site its designation: STB038. Overall, the site's longitudinal extents stretched 117 feet south from a wooden stock anchor at the shipwreck's north end. A hawse pipe and chain next to the anchor confirmed that the vessel's bow lay at this end. Its paver pile spread 100 feet on the north–south axis and 60 feet on an east–west axis. Loops of wire rope standing rigging and chain plates that had once secured the vessel's masts to its hull were imaged along the northern edge of the paver pile. Based on the paver pile's size and historically reported quantities carried by coasting schooners, archaeologists estimated that there were upward of ten thousand pavers on the site measuring, on average, ten inches long, eight inches wide and four inches thick. These dimensions were consistent with historically reported dimensions of pavers used on the approaches to the Brooklyn Bridge and other New York paving projects.[96]

STB038's location on the northeast flank of Stellwagen Bank and its observed characteristics were similar to the historically reported sinkings of

A chalice sponge sits atop STB0038's cargo, while a cusk peers from in between the pavers. *NOAA/SBNMS and NURTEC-UConn.*

three vessels, the *Addie E. Snow*, the *Edwin I. Morrison* and the *Lucy D*. All three schooners carried granite pavers on their last voyages, and all three foundered in deep water north of Cape Cod. Sunk during the *Portland* Gale, the *Addie E. Snow* was the smallest of the three, with two masts, while the *Edwin I. Morrison* and *Lucy D.* were larger three-masted schooners. In the future, sampling the granite cargo may provide the best information to rule out one, two or all three vessels, as all three loaded cargos from different quarries. The *Addie E. Snow* took on its paver cargo from St. Helena Island off the coast of Stonington, Maine; the *Edwin I. Morrison* loaded pavers in Rockport, Massachusetts; and the *Lucy D.* loaded pavers in Rockport, Maine. Current thinking leans toward the *Lucy D.* as the wreck's identity due to reports of its sinking that coincide closely to the wreck's actual position. In particular, a letter submitted by Ensign Everett Hayden of the U.S. Navy to his superiors describing the activities of the USS *Despatch* as it steamed from Newport to Boston in 1888 provided a geographic position for the *Lucy D.*'s wreck. On September 22, the steamship's crew destroyed a navigational obstruction identified as the *Lucy D.* within four miles of the wreck's location.[97]

Shipbuilder George Thomas constructed the schooner *Lucy D.* at his shipyard on Granite Wharf in Quincy. Known as Deacon Thomas for his standing in the local church, Thomas moved his shipbuilding business to Quincy from Rockland, Maine, in 1854 to expand his operation. When the *Lucy D.* slid into the waters off Quincy Point in November 1866, its 110-foot-long hull sported the three equal-length masts of a "tern schooner." Thomas built the schooner for its first captain and owner, Daniel Higgins, who retained ownership and command until around 1875, operating out of Quincy Point. After that time, the schooner was repeatedly sold and changed command before its homeport switched to Boston in 1881. Working in the coasting trade, the *Lucy D.* visited the ports of Philadelphia; Wilmington, North Carolina; Charleston, South Carolina; and Hoboken, among others, while carrying a variety of cargos, including coal, cotton, phosphate rock and bones.[98]

On its last voyage, Captain S. Walls and his five-man crew loaded paving stones at Rockport, Maine, for New York. While sailing south, the schooner sprang a leak on the night of August 11, 1886. The crew abandoned ship eighteen miles east-southeast from Thacher Island and was rescued by the fishing schooner *Wachusett* returning to Gloucester from Georges Bank. Apparently, the *Lucy D.* did not sink immediately; the following day the schooner *Sabao* took two topsails and some rigging from the still buoyant hull floating above Stellwagen Bank.[99]

SAILING TOMBSTONES

ARCHAEOLOGICAL SITES STB032 AND STB042

In addition to the aforementioned granite shipwrecks, archaeological investigation of two other wrecks, STB032 and STB042, revealed the sites to be similarly sized vessels carrying large pieces of granite. Located in 2008 with side-scan sonar, the granite slab pile on STB032 measured 57 feet long by 36 feet wide, oriented on an east–west axis. Fragmented pieces of the shipwreck stretched over an area 130 feet long by 82 feet wide. When archaeologists visited the site with NURTEC-UConn's *Kraken 2* ROV in 2010, they found what remained of the vessel's hull largely buried in mud. While reconnoitering the site, the research team found an anchor chain pile and a fragmented windlass at opposite ends of the wreck. Normally, the co-location of these features indicated the vessel's bow. In this case, the highly concreted chain pile at the shipwreck's east end was interpreted to be the bow, as the windlass barrel could have been moved from its original location by subsequent bottom fishing activities. Adjacent to the chain pile, the ROV imaged the prismatic lens from a navigational light along with deadeyes and sheaves from the vessel's rigging.

Site STB032's cargo consisted of roughly finished granite slabs two feet thick, four feet wide and as much as ten feet long jumbled together in some places and stacked three slabs deep in others. Archaeologists counted roughly two dozen flat slabs during the ROV dive. Interestingly, the survey found one additional large granite block of similar length but pentagonal in cross section with two-foot-wide faces. The shape suggested a keystone used at the top of an arch. The cargo's consistent sizes, smoothed surfaces and sharp ninety-degree angles indicated that it was quarried to specific dimensions for a construction project rather than being grout or rubble fill for a breakwater.

During August 2010, Stellwagen Bank Sanctuary archaeologists used a highly sophisticated synthetic aperture sonar to map the sanctuary's northwest corner, covering a larger area to higher resolution than previously achieved with side-scan sonar surveys. The project located several shipwrecks, including one with granite cargo that was designated STB042. Covering an area sixty-four feet long by thirty feet wide, site investigation with a small Seabotix ROV revealed piled stone blocks covering wooden hull remains. Unlike the flat slabs found on STB032, STB042's angular blocks were roughly square in cross-section. Located at a depth of just over two hundred feet made it the most accessible granite shipwreck discovered so far, but the little ROV's ability to image the site left many questions unanswered.

A cod shelters behind STB032's cargo of finished granite slabs. *NOAA/SBNMS and NURTEC-UConn.*

Partnering with a group of highly skilled technical divers led by Heather Knowles of Northern Atlantic Dive Expeditions, Inc. (NADE) has allowed archaeologists to learn much more about STB042. Working under a memorandum of agreement between NOAA and NADE, Knowles organized a team of technical divers to visit the wreck, document it with photos and video and then report their findings to Stellwagen Bank sanctuary staff. Using rebreather technology allowed the divers to optimize their time spent on the wreck and to maintain a high level of focus for detailed observation at that depth. In particular, the photographic skills of Knowles and team member Ryan King resulted in excellent images from a dark and murky dive.

Following a single dive in August 2014, the NADE research team reported that it had found three wooden stock anchors on the shipwreck. On the wreck's west end, two anchors were next to a wooden windlass barrel and anchor chain that indicated its bow, while the third anchor was nearer to amidships. Swimming around the site, the divers noticed rigging components and highly

Acadian redfish schooling around STB042's granite cargo. *Heather Knowles, NADE.*

durable lignum vitae sheaves scattered between the blocks. A ceramic shard from the bottom of a bowl lay on the seafloor at the shipwreck's east end, indicative of an area in the vessel's stern that housed its crew. Respecting the look-but-don't-touch ethos of Stellwagen Bank sanctuary shipwreck diving, the team left the shard in place for future archaeological study.

Members of the dive team measured some of the granite blocks; they ranged from twenty-two to twenty-eight inches wide, eighteen to twenty-four inches thick and four to six feet in length. The dive team's high-resolution imagery made it possible to compare STB042's granite blocks to those on STB032, revealing that the former wreck's blocks were not as carefully shaped. While having roughly parallel sides, some of STB042's granite blocks narrowed from one end to the other by several inches. Others had projecting lobes or rebates where the granite's cleavage plane was less than straight.

Following the archaeological investigations of these shipwrecks, sanctuary researchers compared the wrecks' locations and observed characteristics with historical research on the granite trade. The shipwrecks' sizes suggested they were smaller vessels, likely sloops or two-masted schooners. Unfortunately, no likely candidates from the sanctuary's known losses matched the shipwrecks' characteristics. STB042's location near the sanctuary's western boundary put it on the route between Cape Ann and Boston and may indicate that the vessel carried Cape Ann granite, but STB032's location in Stellwagen Basin did not suggest an origin or destination that would eliminate other possibilities. STB032 could be a vessel departing Massachusetts Bay with a cargo of Quincy granite or a vessel sailing with Maine granite on its way to New York or another southern port that was blown off course before it sank. Ultimately, the next step in solving this mystery will be sampling the granite blocks to ascertain the granite's origin.

FROM HOOKS TO TRAWL NETS

DEVELOPMENT OF THE EASTERN RIG DRAGGER FISHING VESSEL

The stretch of ocean between Cape Cod and Cape Ann now encompassed by the Stellwagen Bank sanctuary first gained European notice as a result of its tremendous piscine abundance. Since that time, fishing, more than any other human activity, has created the sanctuary we know today. Above a background of subsistence and small boat fishing that has persisted in the area for millennia, fishing technology refocused effort on the sanctuary's waters. In particular, the transition from hook fishing to trawling changed fishing's potential to affect the sanctuary's seafloor habitat. While the sailing fishermen onboard the loftily rigged schooner holds a mythic position in America's psyche, the democratization of trawling in the form of the twentieth century's eastern rig dragger is the unheralded story most important to the sanctuary's maritime heritage.

BOUNTY OF THE SEA

Fishing has been one of the principal activities of people living in northeastern North America since the retreat of the Laurentide ice sheets at the end of the last ice age. During the roughly twelve thousand years of this region's human habitation prior to the arrival of Europeans, Native Americans gathered abundant shellfish, finfish and marine mammals with spears, hooks and weirs in a seasonal pattern, harvesting food when it was abundant. North America's marine resources were forever changed by the settlement of Europeans in the region in the 1600s. Instead of harvesting the area's marine resources for subsistence consumption, Europeans saw the region's bounty of the sea as a commodity to be sold on a world market.

Cod was the fish of choice because of its durability. Its low fat content meant that it almost never spoiled when salted and dried. The inexpensive, highly portable, protein-packed food graced the tables of Catholic Europe, was traded into Africa and nourished mariners on long sailing voyages. European knowledge of northeastern North America developed from the fishing outposts first established in the Canadian Maritimes. Cod became the foundation of transatlantic commerce; by the sixteenth century, nearly 60 percent of the salt cod eaten in Europe came from northeastern North America. Following the established routes pioneered by earlier fishermen, Bartholomew Gosnold led a party of English colonists on the first colonizing voyage across the Atlantic to New England in 1602. While the colony he attempted to establish on Cuttyhunk Island failed, his most lasting contribution to the region was naming Cape Cod after the super abundant fish found in its surrounding waters.[100]

Early accounts of New England describe the region's abundant marine resources, focusing primarily on codfish and great whales but also recognizing the vast numbers of pollock, hake, haddock and salmon. These animals were by no means unfamiliar to exploring European fishermen, and the seafloor topography found on the western North Atlantic shelf was very similar to the eastern North Atlantic. The North American continental shelf with such fishery promise extended west-southwest from Newfoundland to Cape Cod, encompassing shallow sandy banks, rocky ledges, muddy basins and deep channels, with Georges Bank and the Grand Banks receiving the most attention. Gulf of Maine inshore banks also supported tremendous quantities of marine life due to the very high primary productivity of the coastal waters. Encompassing a seventeen-thousand-square-mile area, the Gulf of Maine's smaller sand banks and elevated gravel or rock ledges were ideal habitat for marine fishes. The best known of these areas are Stellwagen Bank and Jeffreys Ledge.[101]

Earlier European fishermen and explorers laid the groundwork for the Pilgrims' landing on Cape Cod and subsequent settlement at Plymouth in 1620. Initially, colonial fishermen exploited the anadromous fish stocks in local rivers in a subsistence pattern similar to their Native American neighbors. However, the arrival of more colonists and the establishment of settlements around Massachusetts Bay with the explicit purpose of market fishing for cod led fisherman farther afield. Higher prices for cod resulting from the English Civil War further spurred colonial merchants to make the investment in fishing and shipbuilding infrastructure. Cod soon became the cornerstone of New England's economy centered on the Massachusetts ports of Gloucester, Salem, Marblehead, Boston, Plymouth and Provincetown.[102]

By the beginning of the eighteenth century, English colonists in North America developed an extensive trading network encompassing continental Europe, Africa and the West Indies with New England salt cod as the basis for exchange for enslaved Africans, manufactured goods and molasses—known as the "triangle trade." In the decade prior to the American Revolution, dried fish accounted for 35 percent of the average annual value of all New England exports and was the single most valuable export commodity.[103]

Between 1775 and 1815, maritime conflict and fluctuating merchant trade conditions reduced New Englanders' opportunity and ability to fish for the international market. Many New England fishermen left the water for agriculture or to become soldiers while others joined privateers. With the return of peaceful relations after the War of 1812, America's fisheries slowly recovered, and its men returned to the sea in even greater numbers. By 1859, the salt cod fishery's peak year, New England's fleet consisted of over 2,500 vessels.[104]

The development of New England's fishing industry was intimately tied with the growth of Gloucester as a fisheries hub. Its protected harbor and proximity to the underwater banks offshore made the city an ideal location for supporting all aspects of fishing from shipbuilding to fish processing and final shipment. As Gloucester's market expanded after 1846 through supplying fresh fish by rail, fishing craft developed to exploit the incredibly rich fishing grounds on the Georges and Newfoundland Banks. Increasingly speedy schooners raced the short fishing season to secure as many trips to the fishing banks as possible. Racing to the grounds ultimately led to the Heroic Fishermen's Races out of Gloucester that pitted American schooners against Canadian schooners for bragging rights and national prestige. This focus on speed under sail led to the construction of glorious vessels capable of carrying mountains of sail and the creation of a complex mythology surrounding the Massachusetts fishing fleets.

Fishing technology remained relatively unchanged for the first three hundred years of European fishing activity on the North American grounds. Until the mid-1800s, fishermen used hand lines from the decks of small ketches, sloops and schooners. In the following years, innovative fishermen spread their efforts over a larger area by using dories, small one- or two-man

Dory trawling schooners at Boston's T-wharf around 1900. *Library of Congress, Detroit Publishing Company Collection, LC-DIG-det-4a17226.*

rowed boats ranging from twelve to fourteen feet long that could be stacked on the schooner's deck. Dory hand lining substantially increased catches, allowing fishermen to fill their dories many times in a day, but it also placed fishermen in greater danger due to separation from their mother ship in fog and bad weather.

Seeking greater catches with less effort, dory fishermen developed tub trawling in the 1870s to put more hooks in the water. Each tub trawl consisted of a quarter-mile-long ground line with two hundred to five hundred gangings—shorter pieces of line with baited hooks—attached every five feet that was all coiled into half of a barrel or "tub." Each dory carried from four to six tubs and two fishermen, while the mother schooner carried between ten and sixteen dories, resulting in ten thousand to thirty-two thousand hooks set out at one time.

The extremely laborious hook baiting process and the bait's cost led Captain Richard Leonard of Boston to experiment with the English method of beam trawling in 1865. Leonard voyaged to Ireland and returned with a large conical-shaped net, held open by a 50.0-foot beam that caught anything that crossed its path. At the same time, Leonard and other investors contracted Dennison J. Lawlor of East Boston to build the 55.6-foot schooner *Sylph*. Reportedly, the schooner was fast and seaworthy, but its beam trawl was deemed a failure after five attempts off Cape Cod.[105]

The next serious attempt at beam trawling occurred several decades later through a joint effort by Gloucestermen Benjamin Low and Captain Alfred Bradford. The partners had Arthur D. Story's Essex shipyard build an English trawling ketch with a steam-powered winch to handle its beam trawl. The *Resolute*'s ninety-one-foot-long hull with plumb stem and a thirty-nine-foot pole bowsprit meant it looked like no other vessel in the fleet when it sailed from the shipyard in October 1891. Test trawls at Ipswich Bay and Georges Bank failed, and its catch realized a low market price, leading its owners to switch to dory fishing after four unsuccessful trips.[106]

Bradford's experiment paved the way for the otter trawl, which was better suited to New England's uneven and rocky seafloor. Instead of a beam holding open the net, otter trawls used two kite-like structures on either side of the net called otter boards or doors. As the fishing vessel towed its net, hydrodynamic pressure pushed the doors outward, stretching open the net. Wooden or rubber disc–shaped rollers strung on the net's footrope raised the net off the seabed and over obstacles. The otter trawl's invention dates to the 1860s and has been variously attributed to an Englishman named Hearden or to Irish offshore fishermen. The English North Sea fleet first utilized the otter trawl in the 1880s, and its efficacy and ease of use led to its widespread adoption in Europe around 1900. Within the first decades of the twentieth century, otter trawling revolutionized American fishing vessel design, propulsion and deck equipment, transforming the schooner fishing fleet into engine-driven trawlers.[107]

THE FISHING FLEET'S TRANSITION: 1900–1930

During the last half of the nineteenth century, fishermen began returning to the near-shore Massachusetts Bay grounds to harvest a wider variety of fresh fish, including haddock, halibut and flounder. Fishermen never abandoned these inshore areas, but railroad connections and fresh fish markets spurred a resurgence of effort in waters closer to shore, which, when combined with technological innovation, dramatically changed the New England fishery during the twentieth century's first decades.

Following Wilhelm Maybach's development of the first four-cylinder, four-stroke gasoline engine in 1890, gasoline engines became a viable power source as manufacturers increased horsepower and portability. Innovative fishermen recognized that the internal combustion engine could diminish the impact of weather on their enterprises—thus, the marriage of engine to schooner, resulting in the auxiliary schooner. Gloucester shipbuilder John Bishop launched the first fishing schooner with an internal combustion engine in March 1900. Built for Captain Solomon Jacobs, the *Helen Miller Gould* initially carried an inadequate 35-horsepower Globe gasoline engine that was shortly thereafter replaced with a 150-horsepower model that drove the schooner at eight knots. It chalked up several very profitable fishing trips that year and into the next before a gasoline leak that caught fire destroyed the schooner in October 1901.[108]

Coincident with the introduction of gasoline engines to the fishing fleet, New England fishermen sought new fishing technology to catch groundfish. Turning again to Great Britain, an investment group comprising Boston fish dealers and bankers purchased designs for a modern steel steam trawler hull and rights to the patented British otter trawl in 1904. Organized as the Bay State Fishing Company, the syndicate contracted Quincy's Fore River Shipbuilding Company to build the first U.S. steel steam trawler, the *Spray*. The steam trawler first set its net in December 1905 and quickly proved its technology profitable, leading to the construction of fifty-five more steam trawlers between 1906 and 1920.[109]

Essex shipbuilders followed the work of their Quincy brethren and began building wooden otter trawlers. While the cost of these wooden vessels was less than their steel counterparts, the cost and complexity of steam machinery made these wooden trawlers affordable only for corporate fishing operations. Ultimately, the Essex yard of J.F. James and Son rendered the wooden steam trawlers obsolete with the launch of the *Pioneer* in May 1918, which combined the efficiency of diesel propulsion and the efficacy of the otter trawl in one package.[110]

Diesel engines offered advantages that led fishermen to embrace these power plants. Developed in Germany in the 1890s, diesel engines developed greater torque at low rpms as compared to gasoline engines and were safer, more efficient and therefore more economical, making them a good fit for the New England fleet. Lastly, a diesel engine took up 50 percent less space and weight than a comparable steam engine, making it very suitable for smaller wooden vessels.

Shortly after the *Pioneer* went into service, Captain Dan Mullins of New Bedford ordered a vessel that repackaged the *Pioneer*'s fishing gear and propulsion technology into a smaller, more economical hull that revolutionized fishing. Named the *Mary* when launched late in 1919, this new vessel variety was the first eastern rig dragger. Contemporaries described the *Mary*, built by Wilbur A. and J.D. Morse of Thomaston, Maine, as a "schooner dragger." Measuring eighty-one feet long, the *Mary* had a bowsprit and a full suit of sails, but its hull was beamier than a traditional schooner, and a small pilothouse enclosed the wheel at the stern. In addition to the dragger's sixty-horsepower crude oil (diesel) engine, two revolutionary aspects of the vessel were its gallows frames and trawl winch, which had not previously been scaled to a smaller vessel.[111]

Following in the footsteps of Captain Mullins, Captain Herbert W. Nickerson initiated plans for a schooner dragger of his own in 1921. Nickerson sought out famed naval architect Thomas F. McManus to design his vessel's hull and shipbuilder Donald M. Waddell of Rockport, Massachusetts, to build it. Departing from his renowned knockabout schooner design, McManus drew up a workmanlike hull similar to the large wooden steam trawlers but scaled to an overall length of 78.5 feet. With a plumb bow, straight sheer and truncated stern, McManus

Provincetown, at the tip of Cape Cod, was once home to a large fleet of eastern rig draggers. *Deborah Marx.*

set the hull style for future purpose-built eastern rig draggers with the *Blanche Ring*.[112]

While the *Mary* and the *Blanche Ring* were purpose built, fishermen throughout the 1920s converted their schooners to auxiliary schooners and added otter trawl gear to fish for groundfish as eastern rig draggers. This process involved reducing the schooner's rig to bare poles with staysails, truncating the bowsprit to a nub and, in most cases, constructing a wheelhouse to shelter the helmsman. Installing a trawl winch and gallows frames also necessitated structural strengthening to withstand the forces generated by towing and recovering a trawl net.

Purely sail-powered fishing vessel construction came to its conclusion with the launch of the *L.A. Dunton* in 1921 from the A.D. Story shipyard in Essex, Massachusetts. The two-masted, semi-knockabout schooner was the last large-sized fishing schooner to enter service without auxiliary power; it received its diesel engine two years later. The *L.A. Dunton*'s design, with its round bow, shorter bowsprit, long cutaway forefoot and long stern overhang, was the epitome of a New England fishing vessel built during the twentieth century's first two decades, but its highly refined sailing design would soon become anachronistic. The subsequent decades of the twentieth century would see the predomination of a new vessel paradigm: the eastern rig dragger.[113]

MECHANIZATION IN NEW ENGLAND'S FISHERIES: 1920–1950

Dragger captain, marine surveyor and historian Morry Edwards characterized eastern rig draggers as "a compromise between the greyhound speed of the fishing schooner and the slow brute strength of the harbor tug."[114] The design evolved in New England's shipyards in response to technological advancements and economic realities. The eastern rig dragger's defining characteristic was its engine-powered wooden hull that deployed, towed and recovered its bottom-tending fishing gear over the starboard or port sides. Reflecting its schooner ancestors, the eastern rig dragger had an aft-positioned wheelhouse containing its helm, associated electronics and captain's bunk. Below decks, bulkheads divided eastern rig draggers into thirds, with the crew's quarters, galley and mess in the forecastle, accessed with a standup companionway; the fish hold amidships;

and the aftermost compartment holding the engine, generators, fuel tanks, batteries, compressors and the engineers' quarters.

At the dragger's bow, a covered forecastle called a whaleback raised the foredeck, adding protection for the crew against sweeping seas in bad weather. At the stern, draggers had either squared or elliptical transoms. The open deck just in front of the wheelhouse trunk held the vessel's trawl winch, powered through a system of chains and cogs connected to the engine or through hydraulics. Other pieces of fishing gear peculiar to an eastern rig dragger included gallows frames positioned along the vessel's side—one outboard of the foremast and one outboard of the wheelhouse. The gallows frames were metal *u*-shaped supports that carried the weight of the doors when not deployed and held the towing wires when the net was in the water. Larger draggers carried two sets of trawl gear and twin sets of gallows on each side to facilitate switching of gear based on stock abundance and market strength. A dragger with two sets was considered double rigged. In general, draggers with single sets of gallows frames had them mounted along their starboard side. If the vessels encountered other vessels head on, they could turn to starboard, as the nautical rules of the road required, without fouling their nets.

Once the concept of the eastern rig dragger took hold in New England, fishermen and shipbuilders further refined its characteristics. The shipbuilder's goal was to build an economical and durable vessel suitable for towing a heavy net but also capable of motoring to the fishing grounds at a reasonable rate of speed. Eastern rig draggers were ruggedly built with deep drafts and round bottoms, with various bow and stern designs that melded the local working water craft construction traditions with powered yachts for plain and practical vessels suited to their task.[115]

Growth in fresh fish processing infrastructure supported the transition to eastern rig draggers and otter trawling. In 1921, the first filleting machine came into service in New England, diminishing the time and effort needed to move a fish from boat to market. Filleting eased the housewife's preparation efforts and also produced processing waste that was ground into fishmeal for animal feed. At the same time, Clarence Birdseye developed a method of quick freezing that turned perishable fish into a transportable and consumer-friendly product. Frozen filets spurred a new marketing strategy focused on convenience and availability to even the most landlocked states, beginning a trend that distanced consumers from the animal origins of their food products.[116]

From the 1930s through the 1950s, naval architects continued to refine the eastern rig dragger's hull design, while at the same time diesel propulsion

Fishermen sorting a haul of Acadian redfish aboard a Gloucester eastern rig dragger.
Library of Congress, FSA/OWI Collection, LC-DIG-fsa-8d32341.

systems, deck machinery, navigation and fish-finding instruments evolved. The most prolific areas of eastern rig dragger construction in New England were Essex County, Massachusetts, and mid-coast Maine. Facilities for the vessels' construction ranged from well-established shipyards with specially trained labor to fishermen's backyards. Historical records indicate that over five hundred wooden eastern rig draggers were built or converted from schooners in New England between 1919 and 1984.[117]

POSTWAR COMPETITION IN
NEW ENGLAND'S FISHERIES

The outbreak of World War II interrupted normal fishing activities and removed a significant portion of the fishing workforce but also generated new opportunities as wartime demands for protein increased and the Great Depression ended. Following the war, New England's fishing fleets were poised for dramatic expansion. Returning veterans had a large supply of surplus naval vessels to choose from, including submarine chasers and coastal patrol craft easily converted into eastern rig draggers. The most significant advancements came from electronics for navigation and fish finding. Sonar development for antisubmarine warfare changed the simple depth sounder into a sensitive tool for locating fish in the water column. Likewise, the development of LORAN, a radio-based navigation system, allowed fishermen to return to a specific spot on the ocean with a high degree of accuracy.

Increasing world demand for new protein sources after World War II led to foreign-flagged fishing vessels entering the North American fishing grounds. By 1960, fleets of German, Spanish, Polish and Russian vessels were fishing off New England's coast, resulting in Massachusetts' catch plummeting. U.S. fishermen saw what they had traditionally considered to be their fish being harvested by massive, subsidized foreign factory ships against which they could not compete.

At the same time, the eastern rig dragger's domination of the New England fishery began to erode with the transition to stern trawling. Steel-hulled stern trawlers, or western rig trawlers, had wheelhouses positioned at the forward end of the vessels followed by winches, net reels and stern ramps. Stern trawling was safer and more efficient, as the vessels could deploy and recover their trawl nets with less risk to the vessels and fishermen, particularly in rough seas. While wooden stern trawlers had existed in the fleet for decades, the influx of steel hulls outfitted with stern ramps in the 1970s led to attrition in the wooden eastern rig dragger fleet through sunken and retired vessels.[118]

In 1976, the U.S. Congress passed the Magnuson-Stevens Fishery Conservation and Management Act, which excluded foreign vessel from fishing within the U.S. Exclusive Economic Zone that extended as far as two hundred miles offshore. The legislation created a national program for the conservation and management of the United States' fishery resources to prevent overfishing, rebuild overfished stocks, facilitate protection of essential fish habitats and realize the full potential of the nation's fishery resources. Pushing the foreign fleets out to sea jumpstarted the industry and caused a fishery boom. The new opportunities revitalized communities, and government loans with low financing rates spurred the replacement of older eastern rig draggers with modern steel stern draggers. After a number of good years following the exclusion of the foreign fleets in the 1980s, commercial fishing suffered from overcapitalization due to the attractive incentives offered by the government. Commercial fishing and its supporting industries have slowly declined due to reduced fish stocks and further government efforts to restrict fishing to protect those stocks that have not recovered.[119]

In 1994, Congress authorized $30 million for the buyback of fishing vessels under the Inter-Jurisdictional Fisheries Act. The legislation's goal was to help conservation efforts and provide financial help to fisherman affected by the low stock numbers. NOAA's National Marine Fisheries Service took the lead and created the Fisheries Capacity Reduction Initiative, which sought to buy vessels and groundfish permits from their owners for a fair price. The vessels would then be destroyed or permanently removed from the industry. Between 1994 and 1998, seventy-eight vessels were purchased under this program. The buyback targeted older vessels, such as eastern rig draggers, which were not considered to be financially viable assets to the fleet.[120]

Today, approximately a dozen out of over five hundred eastern rig draggers built are still actively fishing or afloat. These vessels are slowly disappearing as they sink or are scrapped. Currently, the *Evelina M. Goulart* and the *Roann* are the only eastern rig draggers held in museum collections. The eighty-three-foot-long *Evelina M. Goulart* was built by Arthur D. Story in Essex, Massachusetts, in 1927 as an auxiliary schooner and then later converted into an eastern rig dragger. The Essex Shipbuilding Museum acquired the *Evelina M. Goulart* in 1990, and it is on display unrestored in a covered shed near where it was launched. Unfortunately, the *Evelina M. Goulart* has been stripped of its masts, deckhouse, fishing gear, winches, engine and machinery. Many of its hull planks are sprung, and the vessel looks to be suffering from rot. Unlike the *Evelina M. Goulart*, the Mystic Seaport Museum completely rebuilt the *Roann* to become a floating classroom for the interpretation of New England's fishing heritage. The sixty-foot-long eastern rig dragger was designed by Albert Condon and built in 1944 by Newbert and Wallace. It fished out of Vineyard Haven, Massachusetts, and Point Judith, Rhode Island, before Mystic Seaport acquired it in 1997.

EASTERN RIG DRAGGER SHIPWRECKS IN STELLWAGEN BANK SANCTUARY

To date, archaeologists have located and investigated twelve eastern rig dragger shipwrecks in the Stellwagen Bank National Marine Sanctuary, making it the most common variety of shipwreck found thus far. Historical research into the area's vessel losses uncovered forty-five eastern rig draggers that likely sank within the sanctuary's boundaries. The more recent vintage of sinkings and the quantities of highly durable vessel components have made it easier to locate and identify eastern rig dragger shipwrecks. Site preservation varies; some vessels are almost completely intact, sitting upright on the seafloor, while others consist of lower hull remains and an engine or trawl winch. One such shipwreck with more limited hull remains has been identified as the *Joffre*, a schooner-turned-dragger that exemplified fishing in the twentieth century's first half.

HISTORICALLY REPORTED EASTERN RIG DRAGGER SHIPWRECKS IN STELLWAGEN BANK SANCTUARY

NAME	YEAR BUILT	LENGTH (FEET)	YEAR LOST	CAUSE OF LOSS
Captain Drum	1875	77.4	1952	collision
Holy Name	1893	81.4	1960	foundered
Olympia	1900	98.5	1964	collision
Jean and Patricia	1906	78.7	1953	fire
Ruth and Margaret	1914	102.5	1948	foundered
Ethel S. Huff	1916	42.6	1945	foundered
J.B. Junior	1917	60	1953	collision
Alden	1917	104.3	1957	fire
Gertrude Parker	1917	93.3	1946	collision
Joffre	1918	105	1947	fire
Nyoda	1918	71.8	1954	collision
Pauline M. Boland	1925	75.8	1930	fire
Barbara C.	1925	49	1951	fire

SHIPWRECKS OF STELLWAGEN BANK

Name	Year Built	Length (Feet)	Year Lost	Cause of Loss
Helen M.	1926	81.2	1957	foundered
Olivia Brown	1927	84.3	1953	foundered
Jackie B.	1929	77.9	1963	fire
Lassgehn	1930	51	1951	foundered
Rose and Lucy	1930	81.8	1964	collision
Rose Marie	1930	80	1971	foundered
Nina	1933	61.6	1952	fire
Mary Alice	1941	47.7	1952	foundered
Heroic	1941	91.6	1969	fire
Leah F	1942	88.5	1949	foundered
Positive	1942	91.5	1954	fire
Villanova	1942	75.4	1964	collision
St. Christopher	1944	90.3	1946	foundered
Nancy F	1944	68.6	1951	fire
Cigar Joe	1944	73	1963	foundered
Captain Scrod	1944	78	1983	fire
Mary and Josephine	1944	66.2	1984	fire
Vita Maria	1945	89.2	1982	foundered
Maria Rosa	1946	64.7	1990	foundered
Salvator(e) and Grace	1947	73	1966	foundered
Lilo	1948	47	1980	foundered
Nyanza	1948	56.2	1990	foundered
Madonna Della Catena	1950	74	1984	foundered
Edna G.	1950	51.4	1988	foundered
Sea Fox	1953	56.4	2001	foundered
Maria Sicilia	1956	62.6	1982	fire
Racketeer	1956	58.8	1989	foundered
Diana & Mark	1959	61.8	1989	foundered
Frances D.	1960	64.9	1982	foundered

NAME	YEAR BUILT	LENGTH (FEET)	YEAR LOST	CAUSE OF LOSS
North Star	1967	55	2003	capsized
North Sea		71	1980	foundered
Our Lady of the Rosary		57	1982	foundered

THE *JOFFRE*:
A TRANSITIONAL EASTERN RIG DRAGGER

Shipbuilder Arthur D. Story built the two-masted auxiliary gas fishing schooner *Joffre* at his yard on the banks of the Annisquam River in Essex. Its enrollment papers describe the vessel as 105.5 feet long and 25.2 feet wide, with an 11.8-foot depth of hold; it was 140 gross tons with one deck, a plain head and an elliptical stern. Launched in April 1918, Story towed the schooner to Gloucester for its engine installation and fitting out. It was ready to go to sea on May 17, 1918. The *Joffre*'s namesake was Marshal Joseph Jacques Cesaire Joffre, the commander in chief of the French army in World War I from 1914 to 1916.[121]

Designed by renowned naval architect Thomas F. McManus, the *Joffre* was considered a semi-knockabout-style auxiliary fishing schooner. Thomas F. McManus was considered one of the most prominent naval architects at the beginning of the twentieth century. His alterations to traditional fishing schooner design allowed fishermen to more safely and comfortably work at sea while increasing sailing speed to and from the fishing grounds. In addition to the *Joffre*, McManus also designed the National Historic Landmark schooner *L.A. Dunton*. In fact, Arthur D. Story built the schooner in 1921 off the lines of the *Joffre*. Currently, the Mystic Seaport Museum exhibits the schooner *L.A. Dunton*, allowing visitors to walk its decks.[122]

Arthur D. Story was a sixth-generation shipbuilder whose yard built 409 vessels between 1880 and 1932. Story was best known for his fishing schooners and in particular the racing fishing schooners that competed against the Canadians in the Fisherman's Cup Races. Arthur D. Story's résumé included the most famous Gloucester schooner of all, the *Gertrude L. Thebaud*, which raced against the Canadian challenger *Bluenose* throughout the 1930s for the International Fisherman's Trophy.[123]

Once the *Joffre*'s engine was installed, the Fred L. Davis Company of Gloucester put Captain Elroy Prior in charge of its new vessel. Like many

The eastern rig dragger *Joffre*, seen here in Gloucester Harbor, underwent several modifications following its launch as an auxiliary schooner in 1918. *From the* Atlantic Fisherman, *November 1943.*

other auxiliary schooners built in the Cape Ann shipyards, the *Joffre* was intended for the mackerel seine fishery, where it was expected to sail to the fishing grounds and then use its auxiliary engine to ensnare the schooling mackerel. Captain Prior took the *Joffre* on its first fishing trip off Nantucket near the South Shoal Lightship. On July 15, 1918, the auxiliary schooner arrived in Boston with forty thousand pounds of fresh mackerel and 112 barrels of salt mackerel. Captain Prior and the *Joffre* continued to bring in cargos of salt and fresh mackerel during the summer months. During this time, German submarines stalked the New England fishing fleet, boarding and then scuttling dozens of schooners. The unrestricted submarine warfare caused fish prices to climb dramatically, making the *Joffre*'s landings even more valuable.[124] As World War I came to a close in November 1918, many of the fishing vessels seized for war duty or built for war duty entered the New England fishery. This influx of capacity, especially in the seine fishery, depressed fish prices and likely led to the *Joffre*'s transition to groundfishing.

From 1919 until 1939, the *Joffre* sailed to the Grand Banks and Georges Bank targeting halibut and other groundfish. Its crew caught between 40,000 and 104,000 pounds of fish per trip dory trawling. During this part of its career, the *Joffre* averaged ten trips per year and caught an estimated total of six million pounds of fish, including several record-setting trips that landed halibut worth more than $10,000.[125] The *Joffre*'s halibuting successes resulted in its being considered to represent the United States in the annual International Fishermen's Cup Races in 1920 and 1921.[126] The races, held between 1920 and 1938, reprised the competition of the 1907 Fisherman's Race but pitted U.S. fishing schooners against Canadian fishing schooners for bragging rights. While the *Joffre* was not chosen for the races by the selection committee, its consideration to represent the United States was a testament to its designer, builder, captain and crew.

In 1939, Simon P. Theriault, the *Joffre*'s captain and owner, reconfigured his vessel from a dory trawler to eastern rig dragger and moved its homeport from Boston to Gloucester. Its target species also changed from halibut to redfish, reflecting changes in fish resources and market conditions.[127] The *Joffre*'s entrance into that fishery coincided with a period of increasing redfish landings to feed civilians and soldiers fighting the Axis powers in Europe.

Four years later, Theriault extensively overhauled and repowered the *Joffre* at the Camden Shipbuilding and Marine Railway Company in Camden, Maine. The shipyard rebuilt the dragger from its waterline up, cutting back its original overhanging counter stern and replacing it with a transom-style stern. The vessel's profile changed significantly with the addition of a new wheelhouse and an enclosed engine room companionway. The yard also outfitted the dragger with a new Fairbanks Morse 320-horsepower, eight-cylinder model 35F10 diesel engine and a new Hyde propeller. The *Joffre* continued to pursue groundfish out of Gloucester after its refit. During 1946 alone, the vessel made seventeen trips and landed in excess of 2,273,700 pounds of redfish, haddock, pollock and cod.[128]

The following summer, at the tail end of a ten-day offshore fishing trip to Banquereau, or "Quero" Bank, the *Joffre*'s luck ran out. Loaded with 143,000 pounds of redfish and five swordfish, the *Joffre*'s crew anticipated a substantial paycheck for their efforts. Nearing Gloucester on August 9, 1947, a fire started in the engine's manifold around 11:30 p.m. and quickly enveloped the wheelhouse. Below decks, the fire burned through the water pump belts, rendering it useless for firefighting. Luckily for the crew, the *Joffre* had been sword fishing that day and had two dories standing by on deck. Captain Theriault and his nine-man crew, consisting of engineer Frank Parsons, second engineer Clifford E. Smith, cook Freeman A. Frelick, Burton Holliday, William Ryan, Millard L. Cambell, George Edgar Hubbard, Manley P. Gray and Cass Isaacs, abandoned ship into the dories as a series of small explosions shook the dragger. None of the crew members received injuries as they abandoned ship.

Crewmen in one dory rowed eighteen miles to shore and landed in Gloucester at 6:00 a.m. on August 10. Meanwhile, the small trawler *Maria Giuseppi* encountered the captain and several crewmen in the second dory as they rowed toward Gloucester. The crew remained with the *Maria Giuseppi*, while Captain Theriault boarded the dragger *Superior* and returned to the *Joffre*'s burning hull. He secured a towline to the *Joffre* in an attempt to tow it to Gloucester but found that the vessel had too much water onboard to make significant progress. The *Joffre* finally sank at 8:50 a.m., ten miles southeast by east of Eastern Point. Simon Theriault had $100,000 of insurance on the vessel—little help to the crew who lost their effects and a possible share per man of $230 from the fish caught during the last trip.[129]

THE JOFFRE'S SHIPWRECK

A local fisherman provided sanctuary staff with coordinates for a trawl net hang in an area of muddy seafloor in Gloucester Basin between Cape Ann and Stellwagen Bank. The information led to side-scan sonar surveys in 2005 and 2006 to determine whether the target was potentially a historic shipwreck and warranted further investigation. Following the 2006 survey, sanctuary archaeologists and scientists from NURC-UConn visited the shipwreck with the center's *Hela* ROV, outfitted with still and video cameras and acoustic tracking transponders, to characterize the site's diagnostic features and its extents. Fortunately, the ROV also carried sector-scanning sonar that was invaluable to locate the wreck in the basin's black and murky water. During a two-hour dive, the research team maneuvered the ROV around the shipwreck, gathering information and imaging nearly all of the low-profile wreck. Following the ROV investigation, the shipwreck received sanctuary site designation STB019.

Shortly after arriving on the seafloor with the ROV, the team located the shipwreck's three-bladed propeller, stuffing box, shaft log, propeller shaft and engine, all fully connected at its stern. The vessel's rudder lay immediately adjacent on the starboard hull edge, and its massive eight-cylinder engine sat upright along the vessel's centerline with its exhaust stack broken off nearby. Three cylindrical iron tanks lay adjacent to the engine on the port hull edge; these tanks held compressed air that turned over the engine's cylinders during startup. Archival research identified the engine as a Fairbanks Morse eight-cylinder model 35F10 diesel engine.

STB019's articulated remains measured ninety feet long by twenty-eight feet wide. Along its starboard side hull planking and frames projected at most three feet from the muddy seafloor while its port side frames and hull planking were mostly buried. All exposed timbers were partially deteriorated; however, archaeologists determined its paired frames measured six inches sided, and both outer and inner hull planking was two inches thick. At the shipwreck's southern end, a single iron anchor came into view on the ROV's video monitors within a tangle of disarticulated wreckage at the shipwreck's bow.

While exploring STB019, the project team found a considerable quantity of fishing gear on the wreck. Some of the gear was the vessel's own, while sections of nylon trawl netting likely came from entanglement by other fishing vessels. The site survey located a trawl winch, at least two trawl doors, a gallows frame and a trawl net. The winch lay upside-down forward of the engine, along the wreck's port side, and had two drums and winch heads on either side.

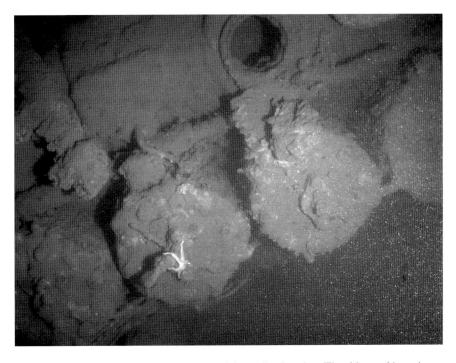

Cylinder heads on the *Joffre*'s large Fairbanks Morse diesel engine. The shipwreck's engine helped archaeologists identify the vessel. *NOAA/SBNMS and NURTEC-UConn.*

Archaeologists compared the sonar- and ROV-derived data to historically reported vessel losses in Massachusetts Bay and the Stellwagen Bank National Marine Sanctuary to identify STB019 as the *Joffre*. The shipwreck's extant fishing gear, such as its trawl winch, trawl doors and gallows frame, clearly indicated the vessel was an eastern rig dragger. Its location southeast from Gloucester matched closely to the *Joffre*'s historically reported loss location in the *Gloucester Daily Times*. The shipwreck's dimensions compared well to the *Joffre*'s historical dimensions, and the shipwreck's wooden remains were consistent with a vessel that had burned extensively before sinking. Archival research focused on the *Joffre* determined that it had the exact model engine as found on the shipwreck. In 2009, the *Joffre* was listed on the National Register of Historic Places. Its shipwreck represents the conversion from a hook-fishing schooner to a diesel-powered trawler, reflecting changes in the fishing industry, both at sea and onshore, that dramatically altered America's relationship to seafood.

THE *EDNA G.*: A PURPOSE-BUILT EASTERN RIG DRAGGER

Whereas the *Joffre*'s shipwreck structure was largely reduced by the fire that sank it, archaeologists were thrilled to find an eastern rig dragger upright on the sanctuary's seafloor that was nearly intact. Historical research following the shipwreck's investigation took several years to identify it as the *Edna G.*

The Morehead City Shipbuilding Corporation, of Morehead City, North Carolina, launched the 51.4-foot eastern rig dragger *Edna G.* in July 1956. The *Edna G.*'s motive power came from a 205-horsepower 6-110 General Motors diesel engine coupled to a three-bladed propeller. Its two 800-gallon fuel tanks gave it considerable range, while 150 gallons of fresh water and 60 gallons of fuel oil for the Shipmate range took care of the crew's needs. Accessed through a doghouse companionway at the bow, the *Edna G.*'s forepeak quarters contained the galley, four crew bunks, a folding mess table with seats and the crew lockers. At amidships, the fish hold had eleven pens for iced fish, while on deck the *Edna G.* had a Model 7233X Hathaway two-drum trawl oriented fore and aft. Its wheelhouse, the nerve center of the fishing operations, had a Raytheon fathometer and Apelco radiotelephone—state-of-the-art fish-finding and communication capabilities at the time. The captain's quarters in the wheelhouse consisted

Eastern rig dragger the *Edna G.* on its sea trial off North Carolina. National Fisherman, *July 1956.*

of a single built-in bunk with drawers underneath. A structure called a turtleback attached to the aft side of the *Edna G.*'s wheelhouse held its head.[130]

The Morehead City Shipbuilding Corporation opened for business in 1950 at a location that had served as a shipyard since 1909. The company offered wooden fishing vessels in fifty-, fifty-five-, sixty- and sixty-eight-foot lengths and was known for building western rig fishing vessels with the pilothouse at the bow and a large deck space in the stern. Trade publications described them as "Hatteras Trawlers," designed and outfitted mostly for the southern shrimp industry. The company occasionally built eastern rig vessels like the *Edna G.* but did not have specific eastern rig dragger plans. Instead, the yard adapted its western rig plans to build draggers for the northern market.[131]

The July 1956 issue of *National Fisherman* included an article on the *Edna G.*'s launch and sea trial. The publication reported that Guido Grasso of New Haven, Connecticut, ordered the *Edna G.* Apparently, Grasso never took delivery of the dragger, as the 1957 edition of *Merchant Vessels of the United States* listed Earl H. Holton of Vandemere, North Carolina, as the owner and its homeport as Morehead City, North Carolina.

Earl H. Holton owned the *Edna G.* from 1956 until 1972. When Holton bought the dragger, he owned eight other vessels fishing for flounder, shrimp, sea trout and croakers. Not only a fleet owner, Holton was also the first president of the North Carolina Fisheries Association and founded the Pamlico Packing Company in Vandemere. The packing company processed oysters, fish and shrimp. In addition to seafood processing, Holton operated an ice plant, a trucking business, a dehydrating company and a boat maintenance shop. His business spanned the entire fishing industry from outfitting the vessels to finished products like frozen shrimp and animal feed.[132] During the last two years of its southern career, from 1972 to 1973, the *Edna G.*'s ownership changed to Trawler Edna G., Incorporated; however, its homeport remained Morehead City.

In 1974, Joseph S. Lochirco bought the *Edna G.* and motored it north to Portland so it could finally join the New England fishery. Three years later, the *Edna G.*'s homeport changed to Gloucester under the corporation Boat Edna G., Inc. Gloucestermen Joseph Lochirco, Salvatore Sciortino and Pasquale Vitale captained the *Edna G.* from 1977 until 1988, when Antonio Romeo purchased the vessel.[133]

The *Edna G.* met its end eighteen miles southeast of Gloucester on June 30, 1988. Captain and owner Antonio Romeo and his brother, Giuseppe Romeo, were setting out the dragger's net around 5:30 a.m. when they heard a strange noise from the engine room. Looking below, they found that water had already risen above the engine. The brothers immediately radioed the U.S. Coast Guard for help; the fishing vessel *Padre Pio* picked up the call and headed toward the *Edna G.* The Gloucester-based Coast Guard forty-one-foot utility boat departed the harbor shortly before six o'clock, and less than ten minutes later, the *Padre Pio* reported that the *Edna G.* had sunk and that the Romeos were safe in a sixteen-foot skiff. The *Padre Pio* picked up the Romeos and transferred them to the Coast Guard utility boat when it arrived. By half past eight o'clock, the two fishermen were back on shore and offered no comment to the *Gloucester Daily Times* reporter about the cause of the sinking.[134]

THE *EDNA G.*'S SHIPWRECK

SBNMS staff located archaeological site STB009 with side-scan sonar in 2002 while surveying an area with several historically reported vessel losses. Side-scan sonar imagery indicated that STB009 was a potential sanctuary historical resource; therefore, sanctuary archaeologists and scientists from NURC-UConn returned to the site in 2003 with the *Hela* ROV. During a single two-hour dive, the research team imaged approximately 80 percent of STB009's external surfaces, gathering sufficient information to determine the vessel's characteristics and extents.

STB009's articulated remains measured fifty-four feet long by sixteen feet wide with twelve feet of vertical relief above the sediment as determined from side-scan sonar data. The shipwreck's longitudinal axis was oriented north–south with its bow facing south. The wreck's hull was found to be nearly intact aside from a large hole in its portside hull near the engine room. Only its bulwarks and decking covering its lazarette were missing.

Encrusting invertebrates partially covered the wreck's white-painted wheelhouse. Its faceted front side held four rectangular windows framing the captain's view of his deck. The open port side doorway allowed a view inside the wheelhouse, where the vessel's helm was still in place along with a radiator on the back wall just inside the door. A large iron bit at the vessel's bow provided a secure mooring structure, and two hatch openings along the centerline provided access to the crew quarters and fish hold below deck.

The site survey found a considerable quantity of fishing gear on STB009. The vessel's own trawl net was partially suspended by its net floats along its starboard side, while additional trawl netting and entangled gill nets likely came from post-sinking fishing activities by other vessels. STB009's double drum trawl winch was oriented fore and aft, forward of the pilothouse, along the vessel's port side. Both starboard gallows frames and the vessel's trawl doors were missing, but even without these features, STB009's hull shape, layout, wheelhouse and trawl winch clearly indicated that it was an eastern rig dragger.

Archaeologists compared STB009's characteristics to historically reported vessel losses in Massachusetts Bay and Stellwagen Bank sanctuary. The shipwreck's location matched closely to the *Edna G.*'s historically reported loss location in the *Gloucester Daily Times*, as well as a U.S. Coast Guard's vessel casualty report. The site's sonar image measured 54.0 feet in length, very close to the *Edna G.*'s 51.4-foot historically reported length. Furthermore, the shipwreck's extant wooden remains were consistent with historic images taken at its launch in North Carolina in 1956 and in Gloucester. In 2011, the *Edna G.* was listed on the National Register of Historic Places due to its exceptional importance as a remarkably intact example of twentieth-century fishing technology. The shipwreck represents a rapidly disappearing watercraft variety emblematic of the region's maritime traditions.

EASTERN RIG DRAGGERS ACCESSIBLE TO SCUBA DIVERS

Whereas the *Joffre* and the *Edna G.* lie beyond the range of all but the most highly skilled technical SCUBA divers, recreational divers can visit two eastern rig draggers sunk on top of Stellwagen Bank: the *Heroic* and the *North Star*. The Warren Boatyard in Warren, Rhode Island, launched the USS *Heroic* in May 1941. The vessel was built for the U.S. Navy as a coastal minesweeper and designated AMc-84. Its ninety-seven-foot-long hull displaced 195 tons, and a four-hundred-horsepower Atlas six-cylinder HM2124 diesel engine pushed the vessel at ten knots. Armed with two .50-caliber M2 Browning machine guns, the USS *Heroic* and sixty-nine other Accentor-class vessels swept harbors, bays and other protected coastal waters for mines laid by German U-boats during World War II.

The minesweeper received its commission on March 25, 1942, under the command of Lieutenant (junior grade) A.M. White, who took the USS *Heroic* to the U.S. Naval Mine Warfare School at Yorktown, Virginia, and on to Bermuda for training that spring. By July, the USS *Heroic* was back in the Chesapeake, assigned to the Fifth Naval District for the remainder of the war. The U.S. Navy decommissioned the USS *Heroic* in December 1945 and turned it over to the Maritime Commission for disposal in September 1946.[135]

Many fishermen purchased Accentor-class minesweepers for conversion as fishing fleets recapitalized after the war. The *Heroic* undoubtedly fell into this group, although records of the vessel immediately after its sale have not been found. Enrollment records indicate that the *Heroic* was owned by Angelo Bacchi of Boston in 1948 under the name the *Elizabeth B.* The vessel changed ownership to B and C Fishing Inc. of Boston the following year. In 1960, the vessel's name reverted to *Heroic* under ownership of Heroic, Inc. of Gloucester.

The *Heroic* caught fire and sank fifteen miles southeast of Gloucester on August 21, 1969. Reportedly, a fire broke out in the dragger's engine

Divers inspect the *Heroic*'s massive diesel engine. *Matthew Lawrence, NOAA/SBNMS.*

room as it motored to the Georges Bank fishing grounds. U.S. Coast Guard assets responded to the blaze, pouring chemical foam on the fire—to no avail—after the captain and crew abandoned ship and were picked up by the West German fishing vessel *Tiko I*. The fishing vessel's all-Gloucester crew escaped unharmed as the *Heroic* settled to the bottom twenty-five miles northwest of Provincetown in 108 feet of water.[136]

The *Heroic*'s shipwreck consists primarily of its large diesel engine sitting atop the remains of its lower hull buried in sand. Some of the dragger's wooden frames project several feet from sand fore and aft of the engine. A large winch lies astern of the engine at one end of the shipwreck, and several trawl doors lie adjacent to its engine. Scattered amongst the high-quality brass fittings and fasteners used in a naval ship, the *Heroic*'s brass helm survived the fire and now lies on the seafloor. In 2014, sanctuary staff installed a dive mooring on the *Heroic* in partnership with Northern Atlantic Dive Expeditions to protect the wreck from anchoring damage and to facilitate SCUBA diving access.

During the twilight years of eastern rig dragger construction, Royal K. Lowell built the *North Star* in Portland, Maine. Named *Bonaventure* at its launch in 1967, the fifty-five-foot dragger pursued groundfish out of Portland. Under new ownership and homeported in Gloucester in 1975, its

The eastern rig dragger *North Star* motoring through Gloucester Harbor. *Len Parker Collection, Maritime Gloucester.*

name was changed to *North Star*. The varied and many dangers inherent in fishing were brought home to the *North Star*'s crew in March 1977, when an engine room explosion killed one of the dragger's crewmen and damaged its wheelhouse. Unlike the other eastern rig draggers discussed thus far, the *North Star*'s fishing gear was converted from otter trawling to dredging for clams in the 1990s.[137]

The *North Star* met its end on August 29, 2003, when it capsized while dredging for clams on Stellwagen Bank. Captain Samuel Sanfilippo and Bruce Hildebrandt had harvested twenty bags of shellfish during four tows. On the fifth tow around 7:50 a.m., the crewmen reportedly hauled the dredge alongside the vessel and found it full of clams. As they raised the dredge to rail height to be swung onboard, the *North Star* capsized. Captain Sanfilippo was momentarily trapped in the wheelhouse but managed to swim to safety. The fishermen abandoned ship without lifejackets and were rescued shortly thereafter and taken to Provincetown unharmed.[138]

Today, divers can visit the *North Star* on top of Stellwagen Bank at a depth of one hundred feet. Interestingly, the dragger's dredge is caught on several boulders, suggesting that it hung up and capsized the vessel rather than the story reported by newspapers. The *North Star*'s lower hull, engine and propeller are separated from its dredge, deck machinery and upper hull

The *North Star*'s propeller is a great photo opportunity for divers visiting the shipwreck. *Matthew Lawrence, NOAA/SBNMS.*

by more than one hundred feet, almost as if the dragger were split in half horizontally. Cod and goosefish now hide under and around the dragger's upturned hull, and divers report seeing hordes of baby scallops jetting off the seafloor as they swim along.

AFTERWORD

S tellwagen Bank sanctuary's boundary lies three nautical miles offshore of both Cape Ann and Cape Cod, requiring a boat to visit; however, almost one million people a year take whale-watching cruises to view the majestic humpback and other whale species that feed in the area. In addition, SCUBA diving charters offer experienced divers opportunities to visit some of the sanctuary's shipwrecks. For those who prefer to keep solid ground under foot, there are many places to visit shore side to learn more. "Dive in" and visit the museums and attractions around New England that feature exhibits and host events throughout the year on New England's only national marine sanctuary. In the meantime, browse the following websites to learn more about your national marine sanctuaries:

NOAA's Office of National Marine Sanctuaries, http://sanctuaries.noaa.gov
NOAA's Maritime Heritage Program, http://sanctuaries.noaa.gov/maritime
Stellwagen Bank National Marine Sanctuary, http://stellwagen.noaa.gov

The best views of Stellwagen Bank sanctuary from shore are from Cape Cod National Seashore's Province Lands Visitor Center and from atop the Pilgrim Monument in Provincetown. The Province Lands Visitor Center features an exhibit that displays Automatic Identification System (AIS) data depicting real-time shipping traffic throughout Massachusetts Bay and across the sanctuary. Scientists use this information to better protect the whales visiting Stellwagen Bank sanctuary. After climbing the Pilgrim Monument for some shore-side whale watching, be sure to view the historical galleries in the Provincetown Museum at its base to learn about the area's whaling heritage and see artifacts from the steamship *Portland* that washed ashore on Cape Cod's beaches. Not far down the road, more *Portland* artifacts are on display at the Truro Historical Society's Highland House Museum.

Much more can be learned about the sanctuary's maritime heritage through a visit to the Maine Maritime Museum in Bath. In addition to a video display highlighting the stories of Maine-built shipwrecks in the sanctuary, visitors can explore shipbuilding and stories of fishing and coastal commerce. Farther north, the Penobscot Marine Museum in Searsport continues the story of Maine's dominance in the coasting trade with a focus on granite.

Stellwagen Bank sanctuary's largest exhibit is part of Maritime Gloucester, located in that city on Harbor Loop, and features several interactive touch-screen kiosks, video screens and interpretive displays on the sanctuary's marine life and cultural heritage. Maritime Gloucester tells the story of Cape Ann's fishermen from hook to net and even includes a historic marine railway. During the summer months, touch tanks and aquariums give visitors a chance to view sanctuary marine life. Do not miss a sail on the pinky schooner *Ardelle*, an authentic re-creation of a traditional Cape Ann watercraft that plied the sanctuary's waters from the eighteenth century onward.

Like Maritime Gloucester, the New England Aquarium brings the sanctuary's underwater denizens out of the murky depths with aquariums featuring the boulder and sand habitats found in the Gulf of Maine. Cod and pollock swim above lobsters and several colorful anemone varieties. Bright blue wolffish, living in the boulder reef tank, steal the show with their toothy smiles.

Scituate, Massachusetts, home to the sanctuary's administrative offices, has a close connection to the *Portland* Gale of 1898. In addition to the seaside destruction caused by the storm and the stranding of the pilot schooner *Columbia*, the storm changed the North River's mouth, cutting off the Humarock community from the rest of the town. Today, visitors to Scituate's Maritime and Irish Mossing Museum learn about the *Portland* Gale and can view artifacts from the steamship, including a life preserver and cabin doors that washed ashore.

NOTES

CHAPTER 1

1. Bertrand G. Pelletier and Brian S. Robinson, "Tundra, Ice and a Pleistocene Cape on the Gulf of Maine: A Case of Paleoindian Transhumance," *Archaeology of Eastern North America* 33 (2005): 163–76.
2. Thomas Mahlstedt and Margo Muhl Davis, "Caddy Park, Wollaston Beach, Quincy, Mass.: Burial? Centotaph? Cache? or Offering," *Bulletin of the Massachusetts Archaeological Society* 63 (Spring/Fall 2002).

CHAPTER 2

3. George W. Hilton, *The Night Boat* (Berkeley, CA: Howell-North Books, 1968), 11–12.
4. Francis B.C. Bradlee, *Some Account of Steam Navigation in New England* (Salem, MA: Essex Institute, 1920), 54.
5. Edwin L. Dunbaugh, *Night Boat to New England, 1815–1900* (Westport, CT: Greenwood Press, 1992), 29–32, 58–60.
6. William Willis, *The History of Portland, from 1632 to 1864* (Portland, ME: Bailey and Noyes, 1865), 732.
7. Bradlee, *Some Account*, 65–66.
8. *Bath Daily Times*, July 1, 1889; *Boston Post*, September 24, 1889.
9. *Bath Daily Times*, October 14, 1889; Lloyds of London, *Lloyds Register of Ships 1897–98* (London: Lloyds, 1898), POR; Maine Historical Society, Portland Company engineering records.
10. *Bath Daily Times*, October 14, 1889; Enrollment #83, June 10, 1890, Port of Portland, Maine, Records of the Bureau of Marine Navigation and Inspection, Merchant Vessel Documentation, RG 41, National Archives, Washington, D.C.

11. Lloyds of London, *Register of Ships*, POR; *Boston Post*, September 24, 1889.

12. *Board of Trade Journal*, Portland, Maine (May 1890), 27; *Boston Post*, July 7, 1890.

13. Steamboat Inspection Service, *Annual Report of the Supervising Inspector General to the Secretary of the Treasury for the Fiscal Year Ended June 30, 1896* (Washington, D.C.: Government Printing Office, 1896), 29; Portland Steamship Company 1897 brochure, Art Millmore Collection, Weymouth, MA.

14. *Boston Evening Transcript*, November 29, 1898; Peter D. Bachelder and Mason P. Smith, *Four Short Blasts: The Gale of 1898 and the Loss of the Steamer Portland* (Portland, ME: Provincial Press, 1998).

15. *Boston Post*, December 1, 1898; *Boston Evening Transcript*, November 30, 1898.

16. John P. Fish, *Unfinished Voyages, A Chronology of Shipwrecks, Maritime Disasters in the Northeast United States from 1606 to 1956* (Orleans, MA: Lower Cape Publishing, 1989), 148.

17. Steamship *Portland* file, Maine Historical Society, Portland, ME.

18. Department of the Navy, Naval History and Heritage Command, *Dictionary of American Naval Fighting Ships*, "Moccasin," http://www.history.navy.mil/danfs/m13/moccasin-i.htm (accessed December 11, 2014).

19. Department of Homeland Security, United State Coast Guard Historian's Office, *Daily Chronology of Coast Guard History*, http://www.uscg.mil/history/Chron/Chronology_Aug.asp (accessed December 11, 2014); Samuel Barber, "Disasters on Long Island Sound, 1827–1888" *Magazine of American History* 23 (January/June 1890): 483–92.

20. Department of Homeland Security, United States Coast Guard Historian's Office, *Cutters, Craft and U.S. Coast Guard-Manned Army and Navy Vessels, George M. Bibb (1865)*, "ex-Moccasin," http://www.uscg.mil/history/webcutters/Moccasin_1865.pdf (accessed December 11, 2014); *Chicago Daily Inter Ocean*, November 27, 1891.

21. *New York Times*, August 29, 1894.

22. Ibid., June 1, 1896.

23. Ibid., September 24 and 26, 1897.

24. *Portland Press Herald*, "The *Pentagoet*, Little Hope for the Missing Bangor Steamer," December 5, 1898; *Boston Globe*, December 2, 1898.

25. *Boston Globe*, December 2, 1898.

Chapter 3

26. John G.B. Hutchins, *The American Maritime Industries and Public Policy, 1798–1914* (Cambridge, MA: Harvard University Press, 1914), 545–46.

27. Ralph Linwood Snow and Captain Douglas K. Lee, *A Shipyard in Maine: Percy and Small and the Great Schooners* (Bath: Maine Maritime Museum, 1999), 11–12.

28. William Armstrong Fairburn, *Merchant Sail*, vol. 5 (Center Lovell, ME: Fairburn Marine Educational Foundation, Inc., 1955), 3,268–69.

29. Paul C. Morris, *Four Masted Schooners of the East Coast* (Orleans, MA: Lower Cape Publishing, 1975), 1–3, 7, 11, 45.

30. Fairburn, *Merchant Sail*, vol. 4, 2609.

31. *New York Maritime Register*, March 17, 1897; Loren E. Haskell, "The Six Schooners of the First Palmer Fleet," *Down East: The Magazine of Maine* (April 1967); Enrollment

#55, March 17, 1897, Port of Bath, Maine, Records of the Bureau of Marine Navigation and Inspection, Merchant Vessel Documentation, RG 41, National Archives, Washington, D.C.; *Portland (Maine) Daily Eastern Argus*, March 19, 1897.

32. Paul C. Morris, *American Sailing Coasters of the North Atlantic* (New York: Bonanza Books, 1979), 35–37.

33. Enrollment #39, March 24, 1900, Port of Bath, Maine, Records of the Bureau of Marine Navigation and Inspection, Merchant Vessel Documentation, RG 41, National Archives, Washington, D.C.; *Bath Independent*, November 24, 1900; *Portland Evening Express*, November 20, 1900; *Bath (Maine) Daily Times*, November 20, 1900; *Bath Independent*, November 17, 1900.

34. *Portland Daily Eastern Argus*, April 15, 1897.

35. Snow and Lee, *Shipyard in Maine*, 45–46.

36. *New York Maritime Register*, 1897–1902.

37. Russell Doubleday, *A Gunner Aboard the "Yankee": From the Diary of Number Five of the After Port Gun* (n.p., 1896), ch. 18.

38. *New York Maritime Register*, 1900–1902.

39. W.J. Lewis Parker, *The Great Coal Schooners of New England: 1870–1909* (Mystic, CT: Marine Historical Association, Inc., 1948), 52–55.

40. *New York Times*, July 24, 1899; *Bath Independent*, June 7, 1902.

41. *Bath Enterprise*, February 13, 1901.

42. *Bath Independent*, October 13, 1900; June 1, 1901.

43. Morris, *American Sailing Coasters of the North Atlantic*, 57.

44. Parker, *Great Coal Schooners of New England*, 54–55.

45. *Boston Daily Globe*, December 13, 1902.

46. *Boston Herald*, December 23, 1902.

47. Mark W. Biscoe, *Merchant of the Medomak* (Newcastle, ME: Lincoln County Publishing Co., 2004), xvi.

48. Parker, *Great Coal Schooners of New England*, 76; Samuel A. Eliot, *Biographical History of Massachusetts* (Boston: Massachusetts Biographical Society, 1909), 1,638–42.

49. Morrison Bump abstracts of William F. Palmer letter book, letter to George Welt, October 28, 1901; letter to Hyde Windlass Co., April 21, 1902, letters to George Welt, May 22, 1902; June 5, 1902; June 10, 1902; letter to Charles Risley, July 7, 1902, William F. Palmer Collection, Maine Maritime Museum, Bath, ME.

50. Enrollment #1, August 21, 1902, Port of Waldoboro, Maine, Records of the Bureau of Marine Navigation and Inspection, Merchant Vessel Documentation, RG 41, National Archives, Washington, D.C.

51. *Lincoln County News*, August 22, 1902; William F. Palmer letter book, October 6, 1904–January 31, 1905, William F. Palmer Collection, Maine Maritime Museum.

52. Photographs and construction contract for *Paul Palmer*, William F. Palmer collection, Maine Maritime Museum.

53. Parker, *Great Coal Schooners of New England*, 76–77, 92–93, 125–27.

54. *New York Maritime Register*, weekly vessel movements, 1902–13; William F. Palmer letter book, letter to William H. Thayer, April 3, 1908, William F. Palmer Collection, Maine Maritime Museum.

55. Snow and Lee, *A Shipyard in Maine*, 45–46; *New York Times*, October 9, 1910.

56. Ralph D. Paine, *The Old Merchant Marine: A Chronicle of American Ships and Sailors*. (New Haven, CT: Yale University Press, 1919), 185–99.

57. *New York Maritime Register*, April 29, 1903; July 19, 1905; January 3, 1912; May 15 and 22, 1913.

58. *Boston Daily Globe*, January 23, 1907; Palmer Letter Book, letters to Captain Risley, January 24 and 28, 1907; letter to Herbert Damon, December 10, 1908, William F. Palmer Collection, Maine Maritime Museum.

59. Morrison Bump abstracts of Palmer Letter Book, letter to Captain Allen, July 16, 1908, William F. Palmer Collection, Maine Maritime Museum.

60. *Fitchburg (Mass.) Sentinel*, "Ship Burns to Water's Edge," June 16, 1913.

61. Morris, *American Sailing Coasters of the North Atlantic*, 197–201; Parker, *Great Coal Schooners of New England*.

CHAPTER 4

62. Arthur W. Brayley, *History of the Granite Industry of New England* (Boston: National Association of Granite Industries of the United States, 1913), 13, 17–19; Granite Railway Company, "Early Days of New England Transportation," *Granite Railway Magazine* (March 1913): 10.

63. Frank F. Crane, "Quincy's Waterfront," *New England Magazine* 2 (1910): 174; H. Hobart Holly et al., *Quincy Legacy: Topics from Four Centuries of Massachusetts History* (Quincy, MA: Quincy Historical Society, 1998); Granite Railway Company, "Early Days of New England Transportation," 8; Brayley, *History of the Granite Industry*, 45; James R. Cameron, "Solomon Willard," *Quincy History* (Spring 1993): 3–4.

64. Brayley, *History of the Granite Industry*, 93, 84.

65. Barbara H. Erkkila, *Hammers on Stone: A History of Cape Ann Granite* (Gloucester, MA: Peter Smith, 1987), 12.

66. Charles R. Pittee, "Rockport's Old Salts Still Tell Thrilling Yarns of Stone Sloops," *Boston Sunday Post*, April 8, 1945; Charles R. Pittee, "Rockport Stone Sloops," *Yankee Magazine* 1, no. 13 (1949): 38–39, 70; D. Hamilton Hurd, ed., *History of Essex County, Massachusetts* (Philadelphia: J.W. Lewis and Company, 1888), 1,380.

67. Brayley, *History of the Granite Industry*, 113.

68. Hurd, *History of Essex County*, 1381; Erkkila, *Hammers on Stone*, 18; "Stone Pavements in American Cities," *Stone: An Illustrated Magazine* 19, no. 6 (1899): 542.

69. Hurd, *History of Essex County*, 1,357; "Air Power Economy in a Granite Quarry," *Mine and Quarry* 1, no. 3 (1907), 219; Captain Charlton Smith, "One Survivor of the Famous Fleet of Cape Ann Stone Sloops," Stone Sloops Clippings File, Sandy Bay Historical Society, Rockport, MA; Erkkila, *Hammers on Stone*, 27.

70. Smith, "One Survivor"; John S.E. Rogers, *List of Vessels Belonging to the District of Gloucester, August 1872* (Gloucester, MA: Telegraph Press, 1872).

71. Pittee, "Rockport Stone Sloops"; E.D. Walen and Howard I. Chapelle, "Rockport Granite Sloops," *Mariner* 2, no. 5 (1931).

72. *Atlantic Reporter* 37 (1897); Erkkila, *Hammers on Stone*, 38; Municipal Engineering Company, "Paving Blocks from Maine Granite Quarries," *Paving and Municipal Engineering* 4 (January/July 1893).

73. Harry Gratwick, "Heavy Freight: When Vinalhaven Stone Traveled the Country," *Island Institute Journal* 23 (2007): 27.

74. George Rich, "The Granite Industry in New England," *New England Magazine* 5 (February 1892): 748.

75. Ibid., 748–49; Sidney Winslow, *Fish Scales and Stone Chips* (Portland, ME: Machigonne Press, 1989), 21.

76. Winslow, *Fish Scales and Stone Chips*, 28; Rich, "Granite Industry in New England," 751; Thomas N. Dale, *The Granites of Maine* (Washington, D.C.: U.S. Geological Survey, 1907).

77. Zarah W. Hauk, *The Stone Sloops of Chebeague and the Men Who Sailed Them, Also Some Chebeague Miscellany* (Freeport, ME: Freeport Village Press, 1991), 12–14, 59, 61, 112, 165–68, 171–76.

78. John F. Leavitt, *Wake of the Coasters* (Mystic, CT: Mystic Seaport, 1984), 151.

79. Granite Cutters International Association of America, "Report from Mt. Waldo, Maine," *Granite Cutters Journal* 35 (September 1911).

80. Hauk, *Stone Sloops of Chebeague*, 4; Gratwick, "Heavy Freight," 30.

81. Roger L. Grindle, "Bodwell Blue: The Story of Vinalhaven's Granite Industry," *Maine Historical Society Quarterly* 16, no. 2 (Fall 1976).

82. Denie S. Weil and Frank A. Weil, ed., *Stone Slabs and Iron Men: The Deer Isle Granite Industry* (Stonington, ME: Deer Isle Granite Museum, 1997), 54–55.

83. "Granite for Building," *Stone: An Illustrated Magazine* 10 (1894): 171.

84. Deborah Marx, "Historic Granite Vessels and Losses Database," Stellwagen Bank National Marine Sanctuary, Scituate, MA.

85. National Archives Branch Depository, Waltham, MA, Records of the Bureau of Marine Navigation and Inspection, RG 41, Merchant Vessel Documentation, *Lamartine* Enrollment #21, May 22, 1891, Port of Deer Isle, ME; Barbara F. Dyer, letter to the author, November 11, 2011.

86. Barbara F. Dyer, *Grog Ho: The History of Wooden Vessel Building in Camden, Maine* (Rockland, ME: Courier-Gazette, Inc., 1984).

87. *New York Times*, "Yankee Enterprise in South America," November 8, 1852; Robert F. Marx, *Shipwrecks in the Americas* (Mineola, NY: Dover Publications Inc., 1987), 437; *New York Times*, "Recovery of Lost Treasures," August 11, 1853.

88. U.S. Department of State, *Case of the Black Warrior and Other Violations of the Rights of American Citizens* (Washington, D.C.: Beverly Tucker, Senate Printer, 1854); David M. Potter, *The Impending Crisis, 1848–1861* (New York: Harper and Row, 1996).

89. *Boston Shipping List*, April 4, 1860; John S. Emery and Company Records [1857–75], MR125 and MR126, G.W. Blunt White Library, Mystic Seaport Museum, Mystic, CT; National Publishing Company, *Commerce, Manufactures and Resources of Boston* (Boston: National Publishing Company, 1883), 155.

90. Grenville M. Donham, *Maine Register or State Year-book and Legislative Manual* (Portland, ME: G.M. Dohman, 1888), 383.

91. *Rockland (ME) Courier-Gazette*, September 6, 1892.

92. Edwards and Critten, eds., *New York's Great Industries* (New York: Historical Publishing Co., 1885), 223.

93. John L. Goss Corporation Ledger for 1893, John L. Goss and Fred A. Torrey Papers (1885–1950), Special Collections, Raymond H. Fogler Library, University of Maine, Orono.

94. *Gloucester Daily Times*, "Timely Rescue," May 18, 1893; *New York Times*, "Disasters to Shipping," May 18, 1893.

95. *New York Times*, December 31, 1893; *Newark Municipal Journal*, September 21, 1916.

96. "Stone Pavements in American Cities," 541.

97. Everett Hayden, "List of Wrecks and Obstructions to Navigation Removed by the USS *Despatch*, Lieut. W.H. Emory, Commanding," *Report of the Secretary of the Navy; Being Part of the Message and Documents Communicated to the Two Houses of Congress at the Beginning of the First Session of the Fiftieth Congress* (Washington, D.C.: Government Printing Office, 1887), 190.

98. William S. Pattee, *A History of Old Braintree and Quincy with a Sketch of Randolph and Holbrook* (Quincy, MA: Green and Prescott, 1879), 495–96; Joseph M. Larkin, ed., "Early Shipbuilding in Quincy," *The Fore River Log* 1, no. 4 (February 1916), 55–56; American Lloyd's, *American Lloyd's Register of American and Foreign Shipping* (1868–1886); *Charleston (SC) Daily News*, "Exports," March 15, 1872.

99. *Boston Evening Transcript*, "Loss of a Boston Schooner," August 23, 1886; *New York Maritime Register*, August 25, 1886; *Bath Daily Times*, "Wreck of the Lucy," August 25, 1886; *Bath Daily Times*, "An Abandoned Boston Schooner," August 31, 1886.

CHAPTER 5

100. Jeffrey W. Bolster, "Putting the Ocean in Atlantic History: Maritime Communities and Marine Ecology in the Northwest Atlantic, 1500–1800," *American Historical Review* 113, no. 1 (February 2008): 30; Mark Kurlansky, *Cod: A Biography of the Fish that Changed the World* (New York: Penguin Books, 1997), 51; Raymond McFarland, *A History of the New England Fisheries with Maps.* (Philadelphia: University of Pennsylvania, 1911), 31–32.

101. Bolster, "Putting the Ocean in Atlantic History," 19; J.H. Matthews, "Fisheries of the North Atlantic," *Economic Geography* 1, no. 3 (1927): 2,8.

102. John J. McCusker and Russell R. Menard, *The Economy of British America, 1607–1789* (Chapel Hill: University of North Carolina Press, 1985), 99.

103. Daniel Vickers, *Farmers and Fishermen: Two Centuries of Work in Essex County, Massachusetts, 1630–1850* (Chapel Hill: University of North Carolina Press, 1994), 144–48; McFarland, *New England Fisheries,* 77, 309–11; Daniel Vickers and Vince Walsh, *Young Men and the Sea: Yankee Seafarers in the Age of Sail* (New Haven, CT: Yale University Press, 2005); McCusker and Menard, *Economy of British America,* 108.

104. McFarland, *New England Fisheries,* 169–71.

105. Howard I. Chapelle, *The American Fishing Schooners, 1825–1935* (New York: W.W. Norton, 1973), 107–09; Morry Edwards, "The Fisherman's Sea Tractor: Origins and Development of the New England Dragger," *Wooden Boat* (November/ December 1987): 51; Joseph Collins, *The Beam-trawl Fishery of Great Britain* (Washington, D.C.: Government Printing Office, 1889), 400–01.

106. Edwards, "Fisherman's Sea Tractor," 51; Dana A. Story, *The Shipbuilders of Essex: A Chronicle of Yankee Endeavor* (Gloucester, MA: Ten Pound Island Book Company, 1995), 137; Gordon W. Thomas, *Fast and Able: Life Stories of Great Gloucester Fishing Vessels* (Beverly, MA: Commonwealth Editions, 2002), 36–39.

107. Frank H. Wood, "Trawling and Dragging in New England Waters," *Atlantic Fisherman* (January/February 1926): 11; William M.P. Dunne, *Thomas F. McManus and the American Fishing Schooner: An Irish American Success Sto*ry (Mystic, CT: Mystic Seaport Museum, 1994), 319.

108. Chapelle, *The American Fishing Schooners*, 221–23; Story, *Shipbuilders of Essex*, 149–50; Thomas, *Fast and Able*, 85–87.

109. Andrew W. German, *Down on T Wharf: The Boston Fisheries as Seen Through the Photographs of Henry D. Fisher* (Mystic, CT: Mystic Seaport Museum, 1982), 104–06.

110. Story, *Shipbuilders of Essex*, 169–71.

111. *Atlantic Fisherman*, February 1926.

112. *Fishing Gazette*, December 1921; January 1922; *Atlantic Coast Fisherman*, September 1921; Dunne, *Thomas F. McManus and the American Fishing Schooner*, 319–22.

113. National Historic Landmark Nomination, Schooner *L.A. Dunton*, Mystic, New London County, CT, National Landmark #93001612.

114. Edwards, "Fisherman's Sea Tractor," 49.

115. Ibid., 50; Peter K. Prybot, *White Tipped Orange Masts: Gloucester's Fishing Draggers, 1970–1972, A Time of Change* (Gloucester, MA: Curious Traveller Press, 1988), 15–22.

116. J.H. Matthews, "Fisheries of the North Atlantic," *Economic Geography* 1, no. 3 (January 1927): 22.

117. Edwards, "Fisherman's Sea Tractor," 63.

118. *New Bedford Standard Times*, September 25, 2007.

119. Daniel Georgianna, *The Massachusetts Marine Economy* (Dartmouth, MA: Center for Policy Analysis, University of Massachusetts Donahue Institute, 2000), 6; David S. Crestin, "Federal Regulation of New England Fisheries: A Different Point of View," *Northeastern Naturalist* 7, no. 4 (2000): 337–50; National Oceanic and Atmospheric Administration, "Brief History of the Groundfishing Industry of New England," Northeast Fisheries Science Center, Woods Hole, MA, http://www.nefsc.noaa.gov/history/stories/groundfish/grndfsh1.html (accessed 2007).

120. Draft National Historic Landmark Nomination, Fishing Vessel *Roann*, on file at Mystic Seaport Museum, 33–34.

121. *Gloucester Daily Times*, April 17, 1918; Mystic Seaport Museum, *L.A. Dunton* Shipyard Reference Collection, *Joffre* tonnage admeasurement certificate, May 17, 1918, Mystic, CT.

122. Dunne, *Thomas F. McManus and the American Fishing Schooner*.

123. Story, *Shipbuilders of Essex*, 86, 118–19, 354.

124. Thomas, *Fast and Able*, 181; *Fishing Gazette*, July 20 and August 17, 1918.

125. Massachusetts Division of Fisheries and Game Massachusetts Division of Fisheries and Game, *Fifty-fourth Annual Report of the Commissioners on Fisheries and Game for the Year Ending November 30, 1919* (Boston: Wright and Potter Printing Co., 1920), 147; *Fishing Gazette*, May 1921; Thomas, *Fast and Able*, 205.

126. *Boston Daily Globe*, October 24, 1920; *New York Times*, September 17, 1921.

127. *Atlantic Fisherman*, January 1939.

128. Ibid., November 1943; *Gloucester Daily Times*, 1946.

129. *Atlantic Fisherman*, August 1947; *Gloucester Daily Times*, August 11, 1947.

130. *National Fisherman*, July 1956.

131. Carteret County Historical Society, Morehead City shipbuilding newspaper clipping file, Morehead City, NC.

132. North Carolina Fisheries Association Newsletter, October 21, 2002.

133. United States Coast Guard, *Merchant Vessels of the United States* (Washington, D.C.: U.S. Government Printing Office, 1971–84); Charles G. Nicastro, *Iron Men, Wooden Ships: Skippers of Gloucester, Mass.* (Gloucester, MA: Charles G. Nicastro, 1988), 29, 64.

134. *Gloucester Daily Times*, June 30, 1988.

135. U.S. Navy, USS *Heroic* entry in *Dictionary of American Naval Fighting Ships*, www.history.navy.mil/danfs.

136. Paul Harrigan, "5 Saved as Dragger Burns," *Gloucester Daily Times*, August 22, 1969.

137. Prybot, *White-Tipped Orange Masts*, 160–61.

138. Dave Wedge, "Catch of the Day," *Boston Herald*, August 30, 2003; Jenni Glenn, "Escape with Their Lives," *Gloucester Daily Times*, August 30, 2003.

Selected Bibliography

Albion, Robert G., William A. Baker, Benjamin W. Labaree and Marion V. Brewington. *New England and the Sea*. Middletown, CT: Wesleyan University Press, 1972.

Babits, Lawrence E., and Hans Van Tilburg, eds. *Maritime Archaeology: A Reader of Substantive and Theoretical Contributions*. New York: Plenum Press, 1998.

Berman, Bruce D. *Encyclopedia of American Shipwrecks*. Boston: Mariners Press Incorporated, 1972.

Bowens, Amanda, ed. *Underwater Archaeology: The NAS Guide to Principles and Practice*. 2nd ed. West Sussex, UK, 2009.

Braginton-Smith, John, and Duncan Oliver. *Cape Cod Shore Whaling: America's First Whalemen*. Charleston, SC: The History Press, 2008.

Bunting, W.H. *Portrait of a Port: Boston, 1852–1914*. Cambridge, MA: Belknap Press of Harvard University Press, 1971.

Catsambis, Alexis, Ben Ford and Donny L. Hamilton, eds. *The Oxford Handbook of Maritime Archaeology*. New York: Oxford University Press, 2011.

DeBrusk, Skip. *Codfish, Dogfish, Mermaids, and Frank: Coming of Age on the Open Ocean*. Stoughton, MA: Reginald van Fenwick Press, 2007.

Delgado, James P., ed. *Encyclopedia of Underwater and Maritime Archaeology*. New Haven, CT: Yale University Press, 1997.

Dutra, Judy. *Nautical Twilight: The Story of a Cape Cod Fishing Family*. North Charleston, SC: CreateSpace, 2011.

Freitas, Fred, and Dave Ball. *Warnings Ignored!: The Story of the Portland Gale—November 1898*. 5th ed. Scituate, MA: Fred Freitas and Dave Ball, 1995.

Green, Jeremy. *Maritime Archaeology: A Technical Handbook*. 2nd ed. San Diego, CA: Elsevier Academic Press, 2004.

Hall, Thomas. *Shipwrecks of Massachusetts Bay*. Charleston, SC: The History Press, 2012.

SELECTED BIBLIOGRAPHY

Hoyt, William D. *Hanging On: The Gloucester Waterfront in Change, 1927–1948.* Gloucester, MA: Chisholm and Hunt Printers, Inc., 1987.

Melton, Mary. *Lost with All Hands: A Family Forever Changed, The Portland Gale of 1898.* Penobscot, ME: Penobscot Press, 1998.

Morison, Samuel E. *The Maritime History of Massachusetts.* Boston: Northeastern University Press, 1979.

Oldale, Robert N. *Cape Cod, Martha's Vineyard, and Nantucket: The Geologic Story.* Yarmouth Port, MA: On Cape Publications, 1992.

Quinn, William P. *Shipwrecks Around Cape Cod.* Orleans, MA: Lower Cape Publishing, 1973.

———. *Shipwrecks Around New England (Illustrated).* Orleans, MA: Lower Cape Publishing, 1979.

Rowe, William H. *The Maritime History of Maine.* Gardiner, ME: Harpswell Press, 1989.

Small, Isaac M. *Shipwrecks on Cape Cod.* Chatham, MA: Chatham Press, Inc., 1928.

Snow, Edward Rowe. *Storms and Shipwrecks of New England.* Boston: Yankee Publishing Company, 1943.

U.S. Department of Commerce, National Oceanic and Atmospheric Administration, Office of National Marine Sanctuaries. *Stellwagen Bank National Marine Sanctuary Final Management Plan and Environmental Assessment.* Silver Spring, MD, 2010.

INDEX

ABOUT THE AUTHORS

John Galluzzo is the Maritime Heritage member on Stellwagen Bank National Marine Sanctuary's Advisory Council, as well as chair of its Business and Tourism Subcommittee. He is the director of education and camping for the South Shore Natural Science Center in Norwell, Massachusetts; the author of more than thirty-five books on the history and nature of the northeastern United States; and holds several weekly and monthly newspaper columns, magazine columns and radio spots. He is the awards committee chairman for the Foundation for Coast Guard History and served for fourteen years as the editor of *Wreck & Rescue Journal*, the magazine of the United States Life-Saving Service Heritage Association. In 2013, he was chosen by the National Marine Sanctuary Foundation as the Volunteer of the Year for Stellwagen Bank National Marine Sanctuary.

Matthew Lawrence is an archaeologist and maritime heritage coordinator at Stellwagen Bank National Marine Sanctuary. A graduate of East Carolina University's Program in Maritime Studies.

Matthew's research interests are the nineteenth-century American coasting trade, steam navigation and the African slave trade. In addition to the Stellwagen Bank sanctuary, he has conducted archaeological fieldwork at the American Samoa, Olympic Coast, Channel Islands, Thunder Bay and Florida Keys National Marine Sanctuaries. Matthew is an avid SCUBA diver who enjoys underwater videography.

DEBORAH MARX is a maritime archaeologist working for NOAA's Office of National Marine Sanctuaries. She is a graduate of East Carolina University's Program in Maritime Studies. For ten years, her research focused on shipwrecks in the Stellwagen Bank National Marine Sanctuary, but more recently she has been working with NOAA's Maritime Heritage Program. Recent research projects

include the Battle of the Atlantic off the United States' East Coast and Gulf of Mexico during World War II and the World War I United States Shipping Board Emergency Fleet Corporation wooden steamships in Mallows Bay, Maryland. Deborah has extensive experience preparing National Register of Historic Places nominations for shipwrecks and has coauthored twelve nominations that resulted in National Register listings by the National Park Service.